ALEXANDER CALDER

MARC CHAGALL

JEAN DUBUFFET

FERNAND LÉGER

HENRI MATISSE

JOAN MIRÓ

PABLO PICASSO

KEES van DONGEN

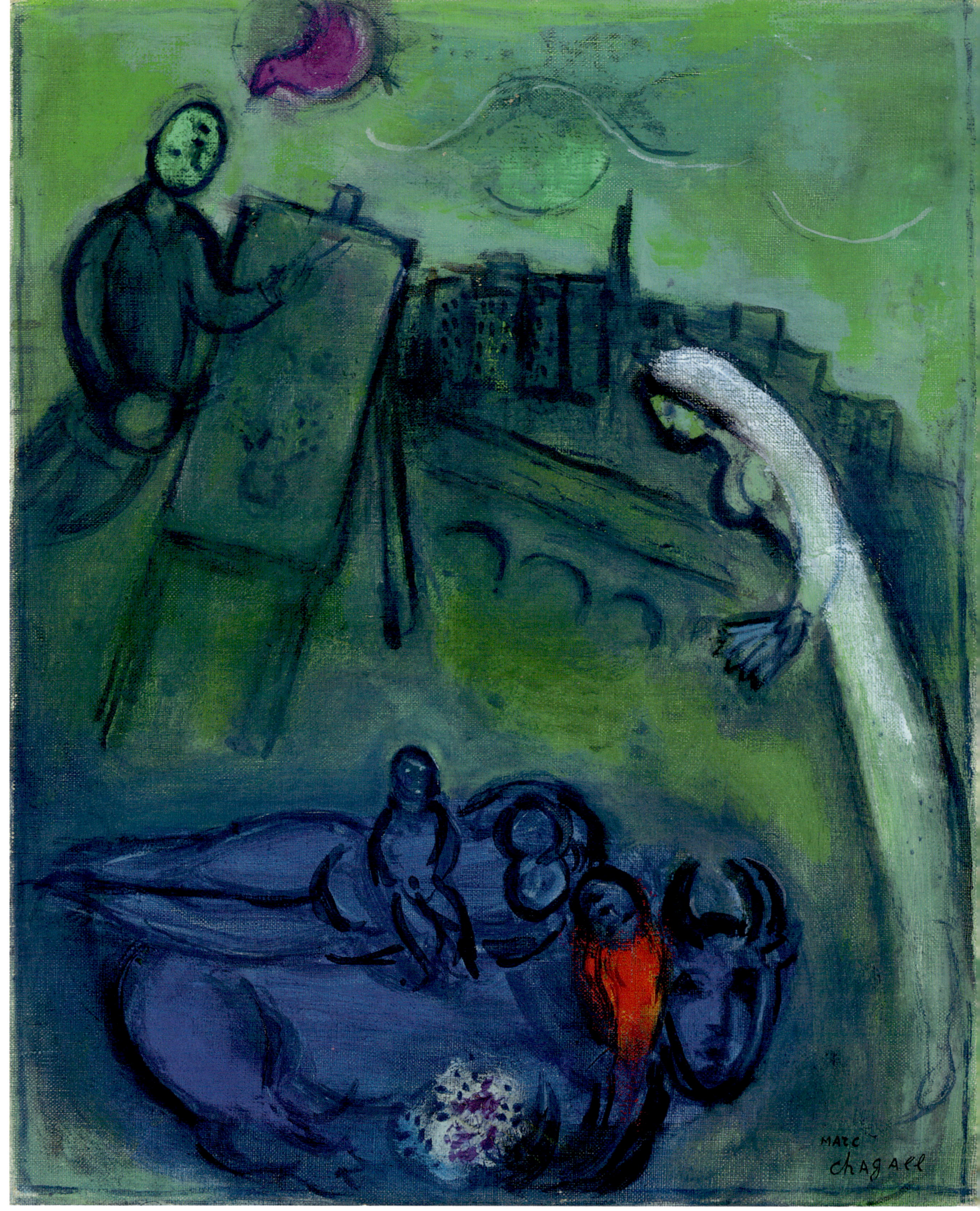

Marc
Chagall

MODERN MASTERS

PARIS AND BEYOND

OCTOBER 29, 2011 THROUGH

JANUARY 21, 2012

HAMMER GALLERIES

ESTABLISHED 1928

475 PARK AVENUE, NEW YORK, NY 10022

ISBN 978-0-615-55329-0
Library of Congress Control Number: 2011941037
© 2011, all rights reserved by Hammer Galleries
Essay and artists' biographies copyright © 2011 Edward Lucie-Smith

Printing by Capital Offset Company, Inc.
Design by Russell Hassell
Photography by Ali Elai of Camerarts Photography, pp. 35, 43, 53–55, 63–67, 75, 87

Reproduction credits and copyrights: p. 14, photo by Keystone-France / Gamma-Keystone via Getty Images, © 1946 Keystone-France; p. 9, 17, © 2011 Calder Foundation, New York / Artists Rights Society (ARS), New York; p. 18, photo by Lipnitzki / Roger Viollet / Getty Images, © Lipnitzki / Roger Viollet; pp. 2, 10, 21–31, © 2011 Artists Rights Society (ARS), New York / ADAGP, Paris; p. 32, © 1973 Pierre Vauthey/Sygma/Corbis; p. 35, © 2011 Artists Rights Society (ARS), New York / ADAGP, Paris; p. 36, photo by Imagno / Getty Images, © IMAGNO /Austrian Archives (AA); p. 39–45, © 2011 Artists Rights Society (ARS), New York / ADAGP, Paris; p. 46, photo by Edward Steichen, © Condé Nast Archive / Corbis; pp. 5, 49–55, © 2011 Succession H. Matisse / Artists Rights Society (ARS), New York; p. 56, photo © Alain Dejean / Sygma / Corbis License; pp. 59–67, © 2011 Successió Miró / Artists Rights Society (ARS), New York / ADAGP, Paris; p. 68, photo courtesy AFP / AFP / Getty Images; pp. 6, 71–81, cover, © 2011 Estate of Pablo Picasso / Artists Rights Society (ARS), New York; p. 82, photo by James Abbe / Getty Images, © James Abbe / Hulton Archive; pp. 85–87, © 2011 Artists Rights Society (ARS), New York / ADAGP, Paris

Cover: Pablo Picasso, *Le peintre* (see p. 80)
Frontispiece: Marc Chagall, *Le Pont Neuf* (see p. 24)
Opposite: Henri Matisse, *Nu couché au polochon* (see p. 50)

CONTENTS

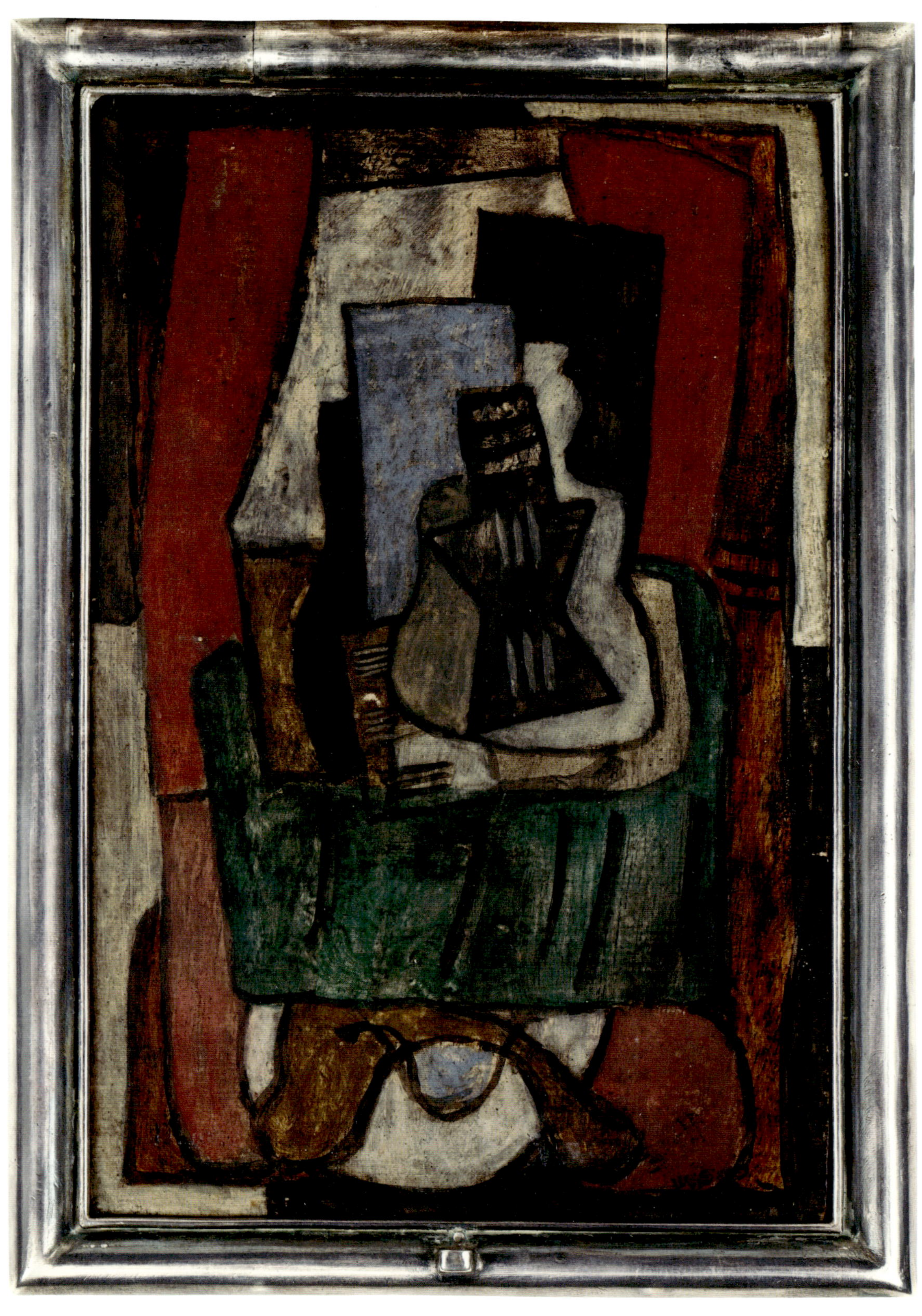

Pablo Picasso
*Guitare sur un
guéridon devant une
fenêtre ouverte*, 1919
(see p. 70)

INTRODUCTION

If you are lucky enough to live in Paris as a young man then wherever you go for the
rest of your life, it stays with you, for Paris is a moveable feast. —Ernest Hemingway

In Woody Allen's charming new film, *Midnight in Paris*, a nostalgic and conflicted Hollywood
screenwriter is magically transported back in time to the "années folles" (the crazy years)
of 1920s Paris. With Ernest Hemingway as his guide, he soon finds himself in the salon of
Gertrude Stein, where he meets Pablo Picasso and Henri Matisse. He attends glamorous
parties with F. Scott Fitzgerald and Cole Porter and has a "surreal" cafe conversation with
Salvador Dali and Man Ray. Many artists, collectors and art dealers have probably had simi-
lar fantasies. I certainly have. I have often tried to imagine what it would have been like to
watch a performance of Calder's "circus" or attend a wild costume party at Kees van Dongen's
studio. Indeed, it is difficult for me to sit at a café in Paris and not imagine a young Picasso
holding court at a nearby table.

For the first half of the 20th century, Paris was the undisputed center of the art world, the
place where any serious artist had to be. Van Dongen came to Paris from Holland shortly before
the turn of the century, and others followed—Picasso and Miró from Spain, Chagall from
Russia and Matisse, Léger, and Dubuffet from the French provinces. As the noted author
Edward Lucie-Smith describes in his catalogue essay, "the result was a mixture between a
stewpot and a laboratory. A stewpot, because all kinds of cultural traditions were blended
together. A laboratory because this is where all kinds of artistic ideas were continually tested
to their limits. . . . The city was a buzzing hive of new ideas." It was in Paris where many of
these artists made their crucial breakthroughs, where they became "Modern Masters."

For this exhibition, subtitled *Paris and Beyond*, we have decided to continue our exploration of this endlessly fascinating period with a new selection of works by Marc Chagall,
Fernand Léger, Henri Matisse and Pablo Picasso. We have also expanded our scope to
include important works by Alexander Calder, Joan Miró, Jean Dubuffet and Kees van
Dongen. Many of these "Modern Masters" explored media outside of painting, and our
exhibition includes sculptures by Matisse and Dubuffet, ceramics by Miró, and an exquisite
"mobile" by Calder. Our exhibition includes works created during this crucial interwar period
in Paris as well as later works produced by these artists after they moved "beyond" Paris.

We will debut *Modern Masters: Paris and Beyond* in our Park Avenue galleries in New
York and present selections during several major international art fairs including the
Pavilion of Art and Design at the Park Avenue Armory, New York (November 11–14, 2011),
the Palm Beach International Fine Art Fair (February 3–12, 2012) and The European Fine
Art Fair in Maastricht, The Netherlands (March 16–25, 2012). We will also present a "virtual
tour" of the exhibition on our website.

This exhibition would not be possible without the continuous support of our Chairman,
Michael Armand Hammer and the hard work of our dedicated staff at the Hammer Galleries.

It is a great privilege to spend each day surrounded by masterpieces of 20th-century
art. I am pleased to present *Modern Masters: Paris and Beyond* to our patrons and friends.

Howard Shaw
President

PARIS AND BEYOND

In the early years of the 20th century Paris became the centre for an international community of artists. Some of them were French, but the city also offered its hospitality to artists from an increasingly wide range of other nationalities. The result was a mixture between a stewpot and a laboratory. A stewpot, because all kinds of cultural traditions were blended together. A laboratory because this is where all kinds of artistic ideas were continually tested to their limits. Nothing like this artistic community had ever existed previously, not even in Rome during the 17th century, when artists from northern Europe flocked to Italy, to complete their technical and intellectual education.

Paris became a magnet for artists from all corners of Europe, and perhaps particularly to those who felt themselves to be disenfranchised in their native countries. Chagall, who was Jewish, had to deal with the discrimination against Jews in Russian society. Miró was Catalan, and belonged to a culture that had never felt itself to be entirely Spanish. Picasso, though not Catalan, had his earliest contacts with the world of contemporary art in Barcelona. Barcelona, disaffiliated from conservative Madrid, looked more readily to Paris than it did to the Spanish capital. Even where this element of cultural disaffection was not a factor, ambitious artists were drawn towards Paris. The Dutchman van Dongen followed in the footsteps of his compatriot Vincent van Gogh. Alexander Calder was attracted by the romantic affection that artistically ambitious Americans had long felt for France. The world he moved in is portrayed in Hemingway's posthumously published memoir *A Moveable Feast.* For Frenchmen, too, Paris was a magnet. Matisse, Léger and Dubuffet were all provincials, who came to Paris to find a wider stage for their art.

A large part of the attraction of Paris was that it was a city of writers and other intellectuals, in addition to being a city of artists. What moved art forward was not simply what took place in studios, but ardent, incessant discussions in cafés, bars and bistros. It was here that the theories that governed the direction taken by new developments in the visual arts were worked out. Painters, sculptors, poets and critics lived in one another's pockets. The city was a buzzing hive of new ideas. While major artists arrived there already equipped with a sense of their own potentiality, it was contact with their peers that provided crucial moments of revelation. Alexander Calder's experience offers a good example. A visit to Mondrian's studio opened his eyes to the possibilities offered by abstract art. Following this, it was Marcel Duchamp who found the name—'mobile'—for the new kind of abstract sculpture that Calder then began to create. Mobiles combine the apparent capriciousness and playfulness of the Dada aesthetic with the discipline and rigor characteristic of

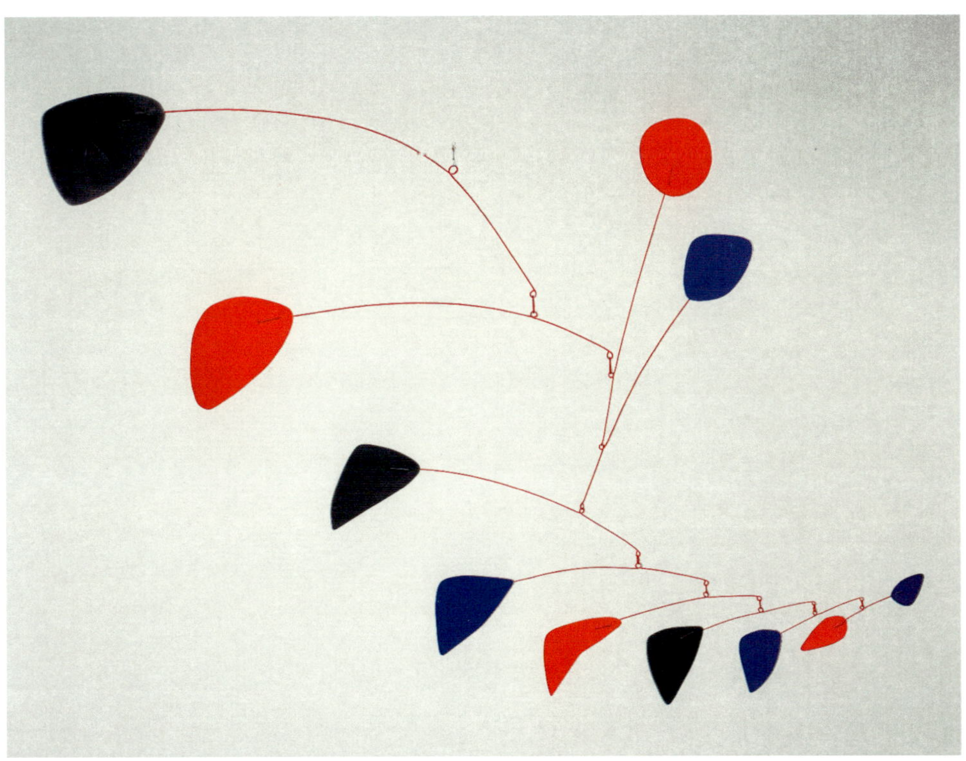

Mondrian's compositions. In Paris, both possibilities existed in the same place. This was by no means the only breakthrough of its kind achieved by the great generation of artists whom we now lump together as the École de Paris. 'École'—'school'—is correct in more senses than one. They taught each other.

Gradually, however, the major figures recognized what were the boundaries of their own creative personalities. They needed external stimulation less, and tranquility to explore their own ideas rather more. The break up of the Parisian community was accelerated by external events. By the end of the World War II it was becoming obvious that the great days of Paris as the place where artists predominently lived and worked were coming to an end. Some important artists stayed, but many more had already departed for other locations. And many of those who were genuinely important now began, wherever they chose to live, to find their most important sources of patronage elsewhere. In large part this was due to the impact of the war itself. Artists who were not French by birth sought refuge wherever they could find it. Chagall, under particular threat because he was Jewish, went to America. So did Fernand Léger. Joan Miró, despite his lack of sympathy with the Franco regime in Spain, returned to his native Catalonia.

The war had other major effects as well. First, it consecrated the idea of Modernism. What the Nazis had hated so much became a touchstone of the innovative liberal culture that had defeated them. When Paris was liberated, Picasso, who had lived there more or less in seclusion throughout the war years, became an instant international celebrity. Modern art ceased to be the plaything of a small section of the cultural elite and became something that interested a much wider public. Old prejudices against the avant-garde were gradually broken down.

This process was hastened by a new fashion for ambitious public exhibitions of Modern and contemporary art. The New York Guggenheim Museum, which opened its doors to the public in 1959, was probably the first statement building that was unequivocally a shrine to Modernism in art. In the post-war years, it was followed by many others, reviving a situation in which Americans were major patrons of the arts, both in the United States and in Europe.

The United States played a major role in the triumph of the artists who had originally gathered in Paris. American economic success encouraged American collectors and institutions to patronize the major names in European art, just as Americans had patronized the French Impressionists in the previous century. The major commissions offered to Léger and Miró in the post-war period are examples. In Léger's case, his association with the United States was one of very long standing. He had already decorated a New York apartment for Nelson Rockefeller in 1931 and had been given an exhibition at the still fledgling Museum of Modern Art in 1935.

The flight from France of a core group of French painters and intellectuals, and their presence in New York during the war years certainly had a profound effect on American art. For example, Léger's role in the birth of American Pop Art should not be underestimated. This does not, however, amount to saying that the École de Paris became in any sense interchangeable with the School of New York. The Abstract Expressionists learned to make daring visual experiments from these French exemplars, but they were less, rather than more, inclined to copy what the Modern Masters did. The time when the still immature Arshile Gorky could say, "When Picasso drips, I drip" was soon over. Personal contact put an end to it.

After the war, while Paris remained a centre for exhibitions and a place where reputations continued to be made—Dubuffet's rapid post-war success, with the help of the leading French literary intellectuals who were his friends, is an instance of this—the leading artists of the École de Paris more and more tended to remove themselves physically from the city.

Miró remained in Spain, living first in Barcelona, then in Majorca. Other leading members of the school increasingly tended to root themselves in the South of France. Matisse had already migrated to Nice in 1917, tired of the privations imposed on Parisians during World War I. Picasso migrated there after World War II, and lived in various locations on the Côte d'Azur—Antibes, Vallauris, Cannes and, finally Notre-Dame-de-Vie at Mougins. After his wartime stay in America, Chagall also settled in the South of France. After returning to Paris from the United States in 1945, Léger traveled regularly to Biot (Alpes-Maritimes) where he had a ceramic workshop. In deciding to settle on the Côte d'Azur, these artists were following an already well-trodden path. Renoir and Bonnard both decided to settle there; Signac spent every summer either at Collioure or Saint-Tropez, where he was visited often by Matisse. Life in the south was the reward that many leading French artists offered themselves once they had begun to make a success of their careers. There is a Matisse Museum and a Chagall Museum in Nice, a Léger Museum in Biot, and Picasso Museums in Vallauris and Antibes.

In the case of Picasso and his contemporaries, there were other reasons for wishing to leave Paris—the increasingly relentless pressure of public scrutiny. Picasso in particular became a major cultural hero, which is to say that he was also an early victim of the modern cult of celebrity. It is not surprising that one of his major themes, during the later years of his career, was life as it was lived within the confines of the studio. While he certainly continued to see old friends, his social life was increasingly constricted by his overwhelming fame.

One thing, however, that continued to link the artists of the École de Paris, even after they had scattered from the city, was the French language. Even artists for whom French was not their first language—Picasso and Miró are cases in point—remained keenly aware of French intellectual values. They could never completely go back to being Spaniards after their years in France. The core members of the École de Paris, wherever they ended up, carried with them a certain intellectual mind-set throughout their working lives.

Edward Lucie-Smith, London, October 2011

Born in 1933 in Kingston, Jamaica, Edward Lucie-Smith moved to Britain in 1946 and was educated at King's School, Canterbury and Merton College, Oxford, where he read History. He is an internationally known art critic and historian who is also a published poet, an anthologist and a practicing photographer. He has written more than sixty books about art, including Lives of the Great Modern Artists, Visual Arts in the 20th Century, Sexuality in Western Art, *and* Movements in Art since 1945. *Lucie-Smith's now classic* Lives of the Great Modern Artists, *first printed in 1999, was recently republished.*

CATALOGUE

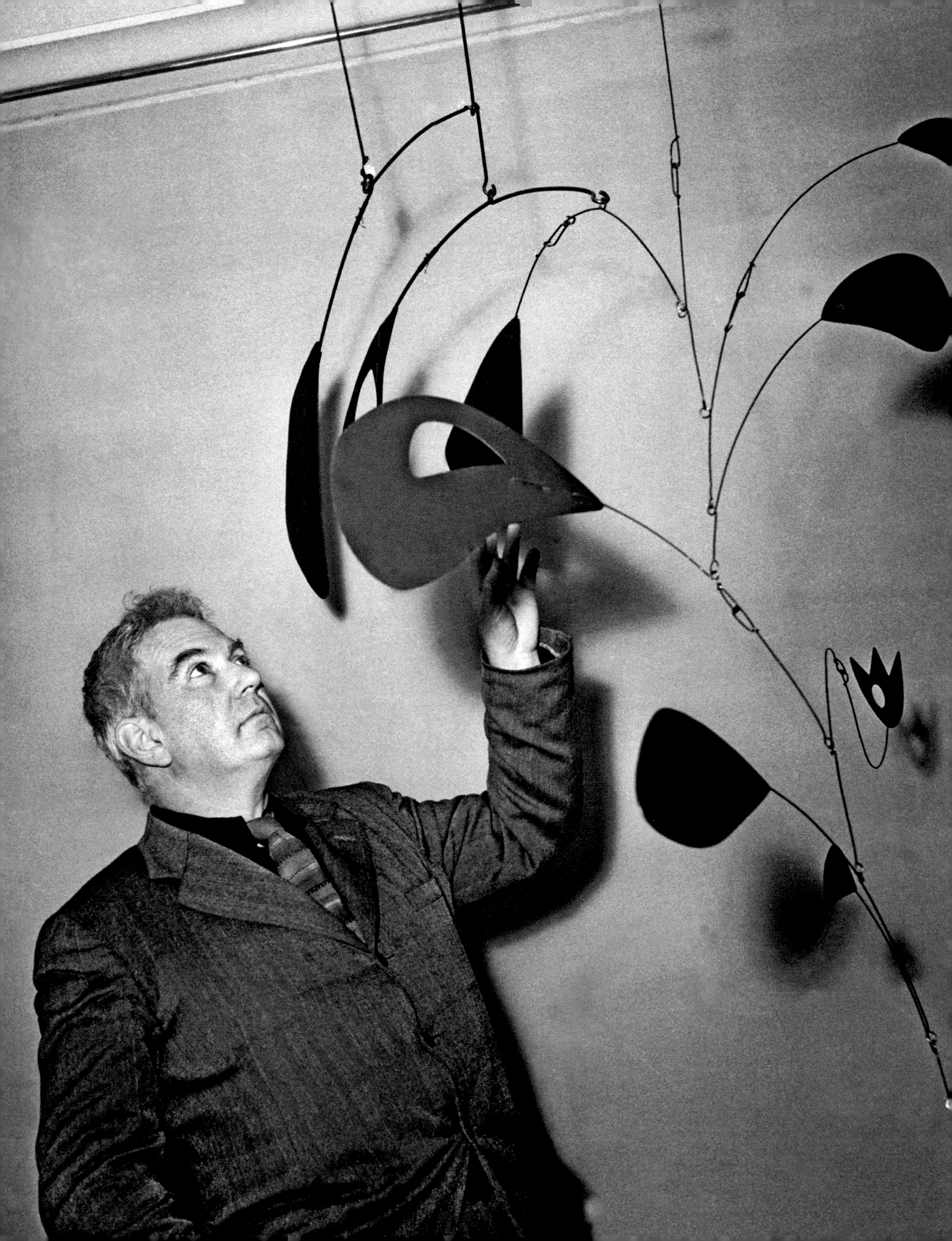

ALEXANDER CALDER   (American, 1898–1976)

Alexander Calder, born in 1898, was the son of two professional artists, a sculptor and a portrait painter. After an education in America that included both artistic studies and mechanical engineering, he moved to Paris in 1926, but always retained roots in America. In the Paris art world he soon became famous for his delightful miniature circus, fashioned from wire, string, cloth, rubber and a variety of found objects. He had a wide circle of friends, including Joan Miró, Marcel Duchamp and Jean Arp. The preface for his first solo show of wire sculpture in Paris, held in 1929 at the Galerie Billiet, was written by the painter Jules Pascin.

A move into abstract, rather than figurative art was inspired by a visit made in 1930 to the Paris studio of Piet Mondrian. This in turn led him towards the development of the works for which he is now most famous—his 'mobiles' (a term invented by Duchamp), consisting of many linked parts, which derived their random motion from the available currents of air. These are generally reckoned to be the most elegant, as well as the most charming of all Modernist sculptural inventions. They offer the simplest possible solution to the concept of 'technological art', and at the same time refer us back to the innocent delights of childhood. The artist had, in fact, begun his career as a maker of toys. The mobiles are the reason why he is now one of the best-loved as well as one of the most immediately recognizable of all American artists.

Calder married in 1931—his wife was a niece of the novelist Henry James—and returned to live in America in 1933. He was given a retrospective at the Museum of Modern Art in 1943, curated by James Johnson Sweeney in conjunction with Duchamp.

After World War II, Calder increasingly concentrated on monumental abstract sculptures, which were now called 'stabiles' to distinguish them from the 'mobiles.' In 1962, he built a studio in Saché, in rural Touraine, France. Most of his monumental sculptures were then made at a workshop in Tours. In choosing to live somewhat retired from the busy intellectual life he had once known in Paris, but still in touch with the French culture that had helped to form his sensibility, Calder followed the example of many of the other major artists of the École de Paris. He belonged to this just as much as he did to the story of American art in the 20th century.

Alexander Calder at Galerie Louis Carré in Paris, November 4, 1946

ALEXANDER CALDER

Red, Blue & Black Cascade
Executed in 1974
Painted sheet metal and steel wire
38 × 52 inches (96.5 × 132 cm)
Initialed and dated on largest leaf: *CA 74*
28036-001

PROVENANCE
Perls Gallery, New York
Private collection, Bloomfield Hills, Michigan
Donald Morris Gallery, Birmingham, Michigan
Private collection, Bloomfield Township, Michigan
Hammer Galleries, New York

EXHIBITED
New York, Perls Gallery, *30 Major Acquisitions*, April 8–May 17, 1975, no.7, illustrated on cover.
Flint, Michigan, Flint Institute of Arts, *Alexander Calder from Michigan Collections*,
    February 20–March 27, 1983, no 9, illustrated p. 16.

This work is registered in the archives of the Calder Foundation, New York, as No. A07732.

"I think that one of the primary models from which I develop form is the structure of the
universe, or part of it. I work from a large live model. When everything goes right a mobile
is a piece of poetry that dances with the joy of life and surprise" (Alexander Calder, as
quoted in Howard Greenfeld, *The Essential Alexander Calder*, New York: Harry N. Abrams,
Inc., 2003, p. 75).
    A classic interpretation of Calder's mobiles was written by the philosopher Jean-Paul
Sartre to preface the Galerie Louis Carré catalogue for an exhibition in Paris in 1946: "A
mobile, one might say, is a little private celebration, an object defined by its movement
and having no other existence. It is a flower that fades when it ceases to move, a pure play
of movement in the sense that we speak of a pure play of light. . . . A mobile does not
suggest anything: it captures genuine living movements and shapes them. Mobiles have no
meaning, make you think of nothing but themselves. They are, that is all; they are absolutes.
There is more of the unpredictable about them than in any other human creation. No
human brain, not even their creator could possibly foresee all the complex combinations of
which they are capable. A general destiny of movement is sketched for them, and then they
are left to work it out for themselves. . . . It is a little jazz tune, evanescent as the sky or the
morning: if you miss it, you have lost it forever. Valéry said of the sea that it is a perpetual
recommencement. A mobile is in this way like the sea, and is equally enchanting: forever
rebeginning, forever new. No use throwing it a passing glance, you must live with it and be
fascinated by it. Then and only then will you feel the beauty of its pure and changing forms,
at once so free and so disciplined. . ." (as quoted in Jean Lipman, *Calder's Universe*, New York:
The Viking Press, in cooperation with the Whitney Museum of American Art, 1976, p. 261).

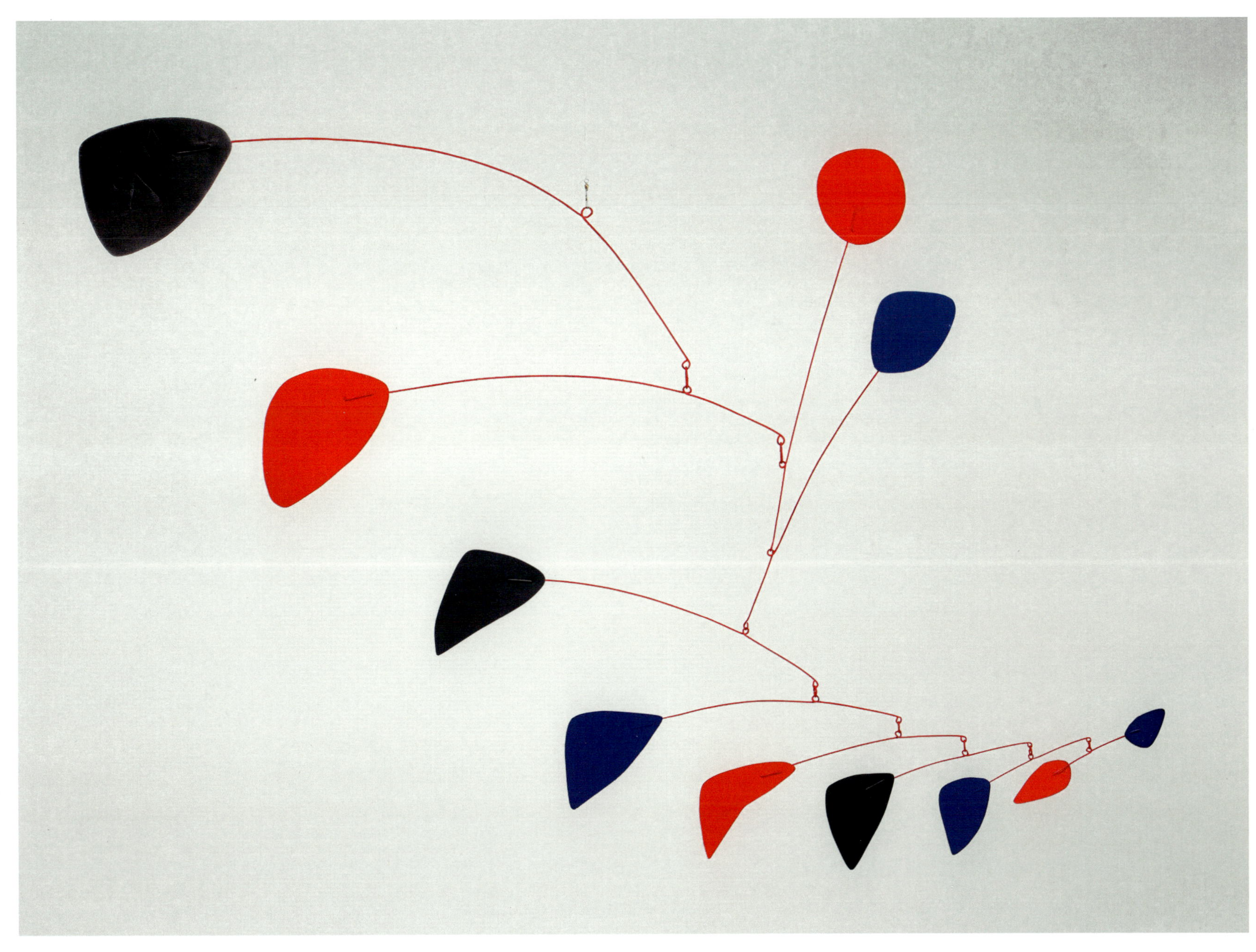

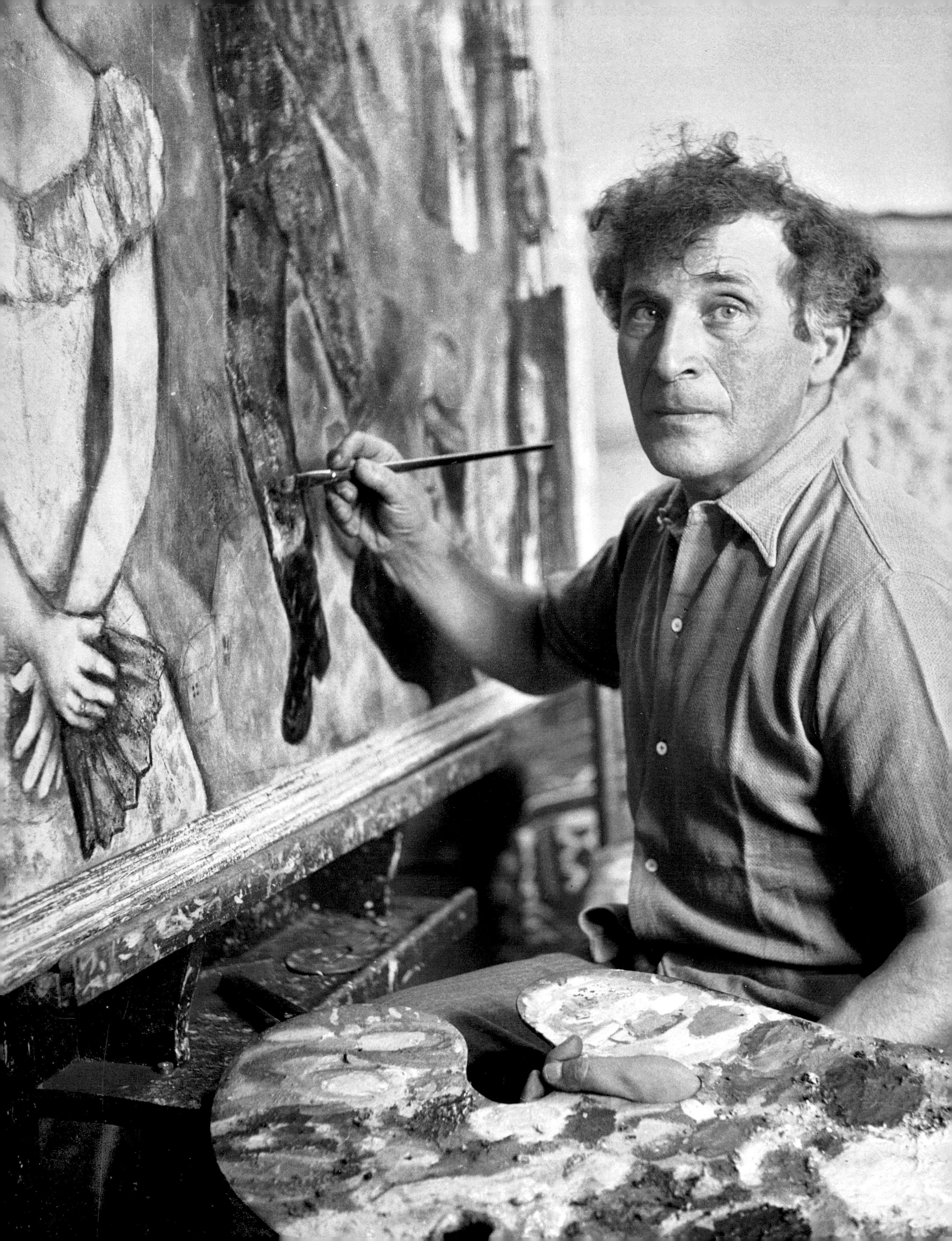

MARC CHAGALL (Russian, 1887–1985)

Chagall wrote an enchanting but wonderfully vague poetic autobiography about his childhood and early youth, entitled simply *My Life*. For all its vagueness and imprecision, it makes it very clear how much his childhood memories fed his work throughout his long career. He was born, the eldest of eight children, into a poor Jewish family in Vitebsk, a bustling town in the Russian part of the Pale of Settlement (the area where Jews were allowed to reside). He was first seized with a desire to draw when he saw another boy in his school copying an illustration in a magazine—until then, he had never seen either drawings or paintings. Eventually he made his way to St. Petersburg to study, despite the difficulty of obtaining a residence permit.

In St. Petersburg he made contact with Léon Bakst, who had very recently become famous for his designs for the Ballets Russes first season in Paris. He decided to follow in Bakst's footsteps and make his way to this magical city. Once in Paris, he quickly became familiar with the leading members of the visual arts avant-garde. He also, thanks to an introduction made by the poet and critic Guillaume Apollinaire, achieved a reputation in Germany. In 1914 he had a one-man show in Berlin, which was an outstanding success. Following this, he decided to make a three-month visit to Russia and was trapped there when war broke out.

With the coming of the Revolution, Chagall sided with the Bolsheviks. By now he was well known in Russian avant-garde circles and he was also known to Anatoly Lunacharsky, Minister for Culture in the new government, who had visited his studio in Paris. Lunacharsky appointed him Commissar for Art in his native Vitebsk, where he was soon in conflict with Kasimir Malevich, whom he had unwisely invited to come and teach there. In 1920 Chagall moved to Moscow, and in 1922, disillusioned with the Revolution and by the dictatorial attitudes of the Russian Constructivists, he left Russia for good, finally making his way back to Paris in 1924. The subject matter of his art, however, remained firmly rooted in the Russian experiences of his childhood and youth.

An additional element was the rediscovery of his Jewish identity, prompted by a contract from the dealer Ambroise Vollard to illustrate the Bible. This led to a visit to Palestine in 1931, where he was present at the laying of the foundation stone for the new Tel-Aviv Museum. He also paid a visit to Vilna in Poland (now Vilnius in Lithuania) where he became acutely aware of the rising tide of anti-Semitism.

During the interwar years he painted some of his most sumptuous works, despite the ever-darkening political climate. The two flower pieces presented here, *Les lys et les bleuets* and *Le soir*, are striking examples of his gift for color. Because *Le soir* was painted in 1938, there is a temptation to see it as embodying a premonition of trouble to come. This is not the case. It is a hymn to the beauty of nature and to Chagall's spontaneous, always romantic reaction to this.

After the outbreak of World War II and the German occupation of France, Chagall waited to leave until it was almost too late. Foiled in an attempt to take passage by ship to America via Marseilles, he, his wife and his daughter finally reached New York, via Spain, in June 1941. Chagall lived in the United States until 1948, before resettling in France where, like many Modernist painters of the great generation, he chose to spend his last years on the Côte d'Azur.

Several additional works belong to the final years of his life, when he was happily settled again in France. They equate his years in Vitebsk, which always remained alive in his memory, with his new existence in Saint-Paul-de-Vence, with occasional visits to Paris. His romanticism and his belief in the power of human love remained undimmed until the end of his life.

Marc Chagall, circa 1934, France

MARC CHAGALL

Les lys et les bleuets
Painted in 1927–28
Oil on canvas
39½ × 32 inches (100 × 81 cm)
Signed and dated lower left: *Chagall Marc 927*
28031-004

PROVENANCE
Jacques Bernheim, Paris
Acquired by the present owner in 1996

LITERATURE
Paul Fierens, *Marc Chagall*, Paris, 1929, no. 24, illustrated.
Franz Meyer, *Marc Chagall, Life and Work*, London, 1964, p. 356, (titled *Lilies and Cornflowers*)
    p. 754 (text), no. 509, illustrated.

This work is accompanied by a certificate of authenticity issued by the Comité Marc Chagall,
signed by Jean-Louis Prat and dated Paris, 5 June 2007 (no. 2007058).

The mid-to-late 1920s were to be one of the greatest periods of success for Chagall, as he
gained wider and wider recognition. It was during this time that he had his first American
exhibition, as well as many other shows in France and elsewhere. It was also important that
in 1927 he signed a contract with Bernheim-Jeune, giving him financial security. During
this period, floral bouquets became a common theme in Chagall's work: "It was in Toulon
in 1924, Chagall recalls, that the charm of French flowers first struck him. He claims he had
not known bouquets of flowers in Russia—or at least they were not so common as in France . . .
He said that when he painted a bouquet it was as if he was painting a landscape. It represented
France to him. But the discovery was also a logical one in the light of the change taking
place in his vision and pictorial interests. Flowers, especially mixed bouquets of tiny
blossoms, offer a variety of delicate color combinations and a fund of texture contrasts
which were beginning to hold Chagall's attention more and more" (James Johnson
Sweeney, *Marc Chagall*, New York, 1946, p. 56).
    In her biography of Chagall, Monica Bohm-Duchen offers additional reasons for the
artist's new focus on flower painting during this period: "One should remember, perhaps,
that flowers were hardly a common feature of his childhood years. Emblematic of affluence,
if not luxury and sensuous abandon, they appear only rarely in his early work, in, for
example, *The Birthday* of 1915. In the very different context of Paris in the 1920s—where,
moreover, from late 1925 onwards he lived close to the magnificent Jardin Fleuriste
(municipal gardens) near the Bois de Boulogne—lovers and flowers abound . . . these
paintings corroborate the artist's claim that 'there lies in the flowers that I paint a subtle
spell which makes them akin to the flowers of God'" (Monica Bohm-Duchen, *Chagall*,
London: Phaidon, 1998, p. 191 and p. 195).

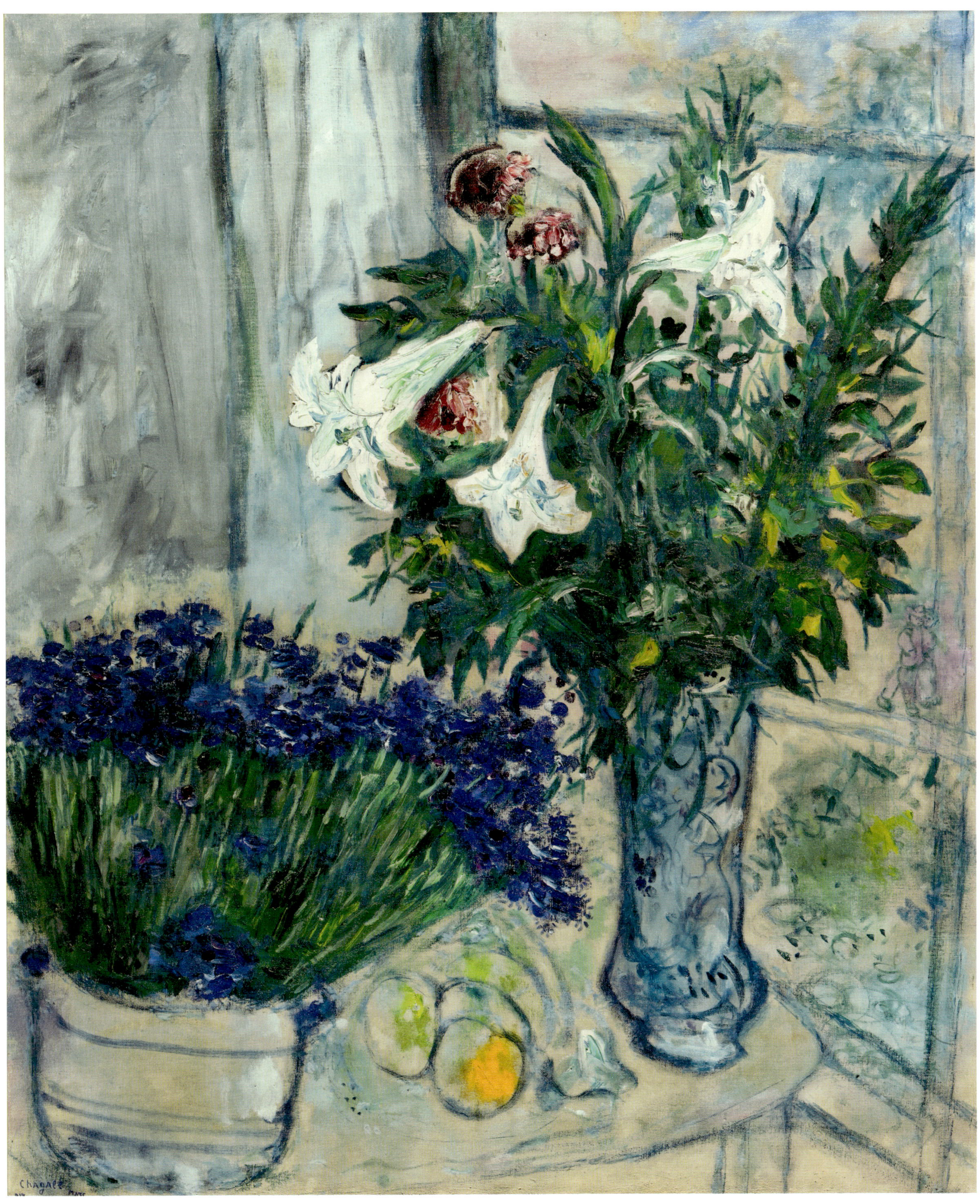

MARC CHAGALL

Le soir
Painted in 1935–38
Oil on canvas
36⅜ × 29⅛ inches (92.3 × 73.7 cm)
Signed lower right: *Chagall Marc*
28036-001

PROVENANCE
Pierre Matisse Gallery, New York
Thomas Laughlin, New York
Acquavella Galleries, New York
Mr. and Mrs. Josef Rosensaft, New York
Private collection (circa 1976–2005)
Acquired by the present owner in 2005

This work is accompanied by a certificate of authenticity issued by the Comité Marc Chagall,
signed by Jean-Louis Prat and dated Paris, 7 October 2005 (No. 2005075).

About works from this period, Werner Haftmann has stated: "During the troubled years
of the late 1930s Chagall also painted some serene pictures, of an astonishingly new and
sumptuous coloring. The harder times became, the more tirelessly he applied himself to
painting and for a while was able to forget the political oppression in his artistic activity.
Whenever possible he stayed outside Paris, so that he and his work should not be disturbed
by the wild rumors running through the city" (Werner Haftmann, *Marc Chagall*, New York:
Harry N. Abrams, Inc., 1984, p. 92).

The iconography, rich coloration and imaginative composition of Chagall's paintings
all contribute to their unmistakable dream-like quality. Chagall himself once wrote of his
pictures: "If someone sees in my art only the search for pleasure, he's free to do so. Free
also to consider how another reality is being involuntarily transformed into symbol, the
illogical and psychical construction of forms and colors. On this point, as on others, I prefer
to keep silent and let people think what they like" (Marc Chagall, as quoted in Charles Sorlier,
ed., *Chagall by Chagall*, New York, 1979, p. 120).

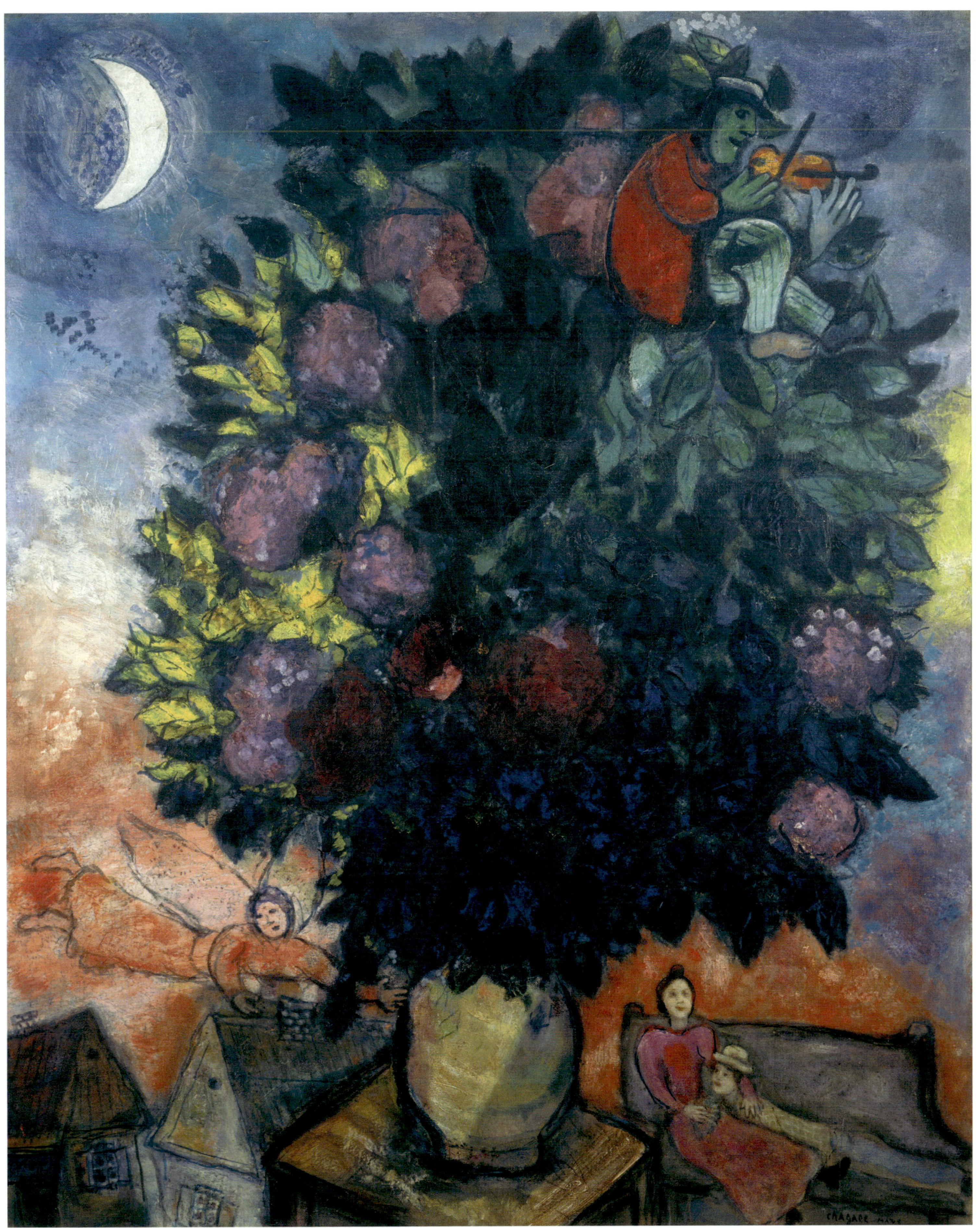

MARC CHAGALL

Le Pont Neuf
Painted in 1953–54
Oil on canvas
16 × 12⅞ inches (40.6 × 32.7 cm)
Stamped with signature lower right: *Marc Chagall*
28031-005

PROVENANCE
Estate of the artist
Private collection
Private collection, New York, 1999
Acquired by the present owner in 2007

This work is accompanied by a certificate of authenticity issued by the Comité Marc Chagall,
signed by Jean-Louis Prat and dated Paris, 19 April 1996.

This work is related to a larger version, also entitled *Le Pont Neuf* and executed in 1953. This
alternate version was exhibited at the Galerie Maeght in Paris along with 28 other works
which comprised Chagall's Paris Series—larger paintings based on sketches he had executed
in Paris in 1946 upon his first return to the city following World War II. According to
Chagall's biographer Franz Meyer, these original sketches were completed "in peculiarly
radiant gouache or with chalks on dark paper. They convey the impression of his renewed
contact with the city, the enthusiasm and gratitude he felt at the time" (Franz Meyer, *Marc
Chagall, Life and Work*, New York: Harry N. Abrams, 1963, p. 529).

 Chagall had been forced to flee France in May, 1941, barely making it out of the country.
He, his wife Bella, and their daughter Ida settled in New York, and it was there that Bella
died suddenly in 1944. Chagall was devastated by her death and immortalized her in many
of his subsequent paintings, including *Le Pont Neuf*; the bride near the right side of the
canvas is most likely a representation of Bella.

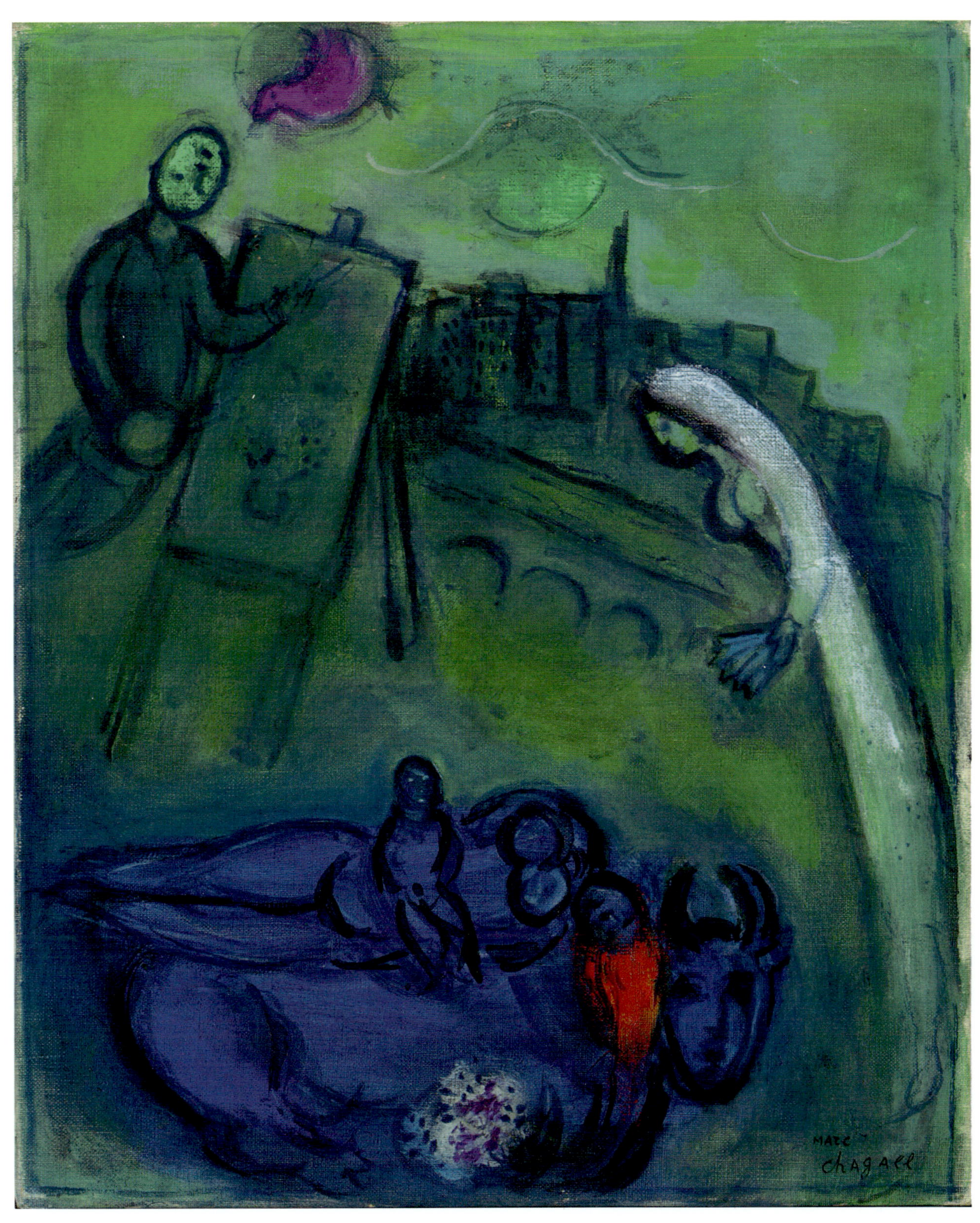
Marc Chagall

L'âne rouge au-dessus du village
Painted in 1978
Oil on canvas
25⅝ × 31⅞ inches (65 × 81 cm)
Signed lower left: *Marc Chagall*
Signed again on reverse: *Marc Chagall*
28031-001

Acquired by the present owner in 1989

This work is accompanied by a certificate of authenticity issued by the Comité Marc Chagall, signed by Jean-Louis Prat and dated Saint-Paul, 2 October 2000 (No. 2000107).

Throughout his career, Chagall's subject matter had been rooted in recollections of his youth in Old Russia and in celebrations of his love for his first wife Bella. Yet Chagall refused "to explain his symbolism or to let others explain it . . . What do those objects that frequent his canvases mean to him, the cows, clocks, donkeys, Eiffel Towers with and without boots on? If color is so important, what does his red signify, or his pale and dark blues . . . ? 'Judge me by form and colour, by my philosophy, not by the separate symbols,' he answers. 'One can see all the questions and answers in the pictures themselves. Everyone can see them in his own way, interpret what he sees and how he sees. . . . For the Cubists a painting was a surface covered with forms in a certain order. For me a picture is a surface covered with representations of things (objects, animals, human beings) in a certain order in which logic and illustration have no importance. The visual effect of the composition is what is paramount'" (as quoted in "Chagall 'over the Roofs of the World'" by Norbert Lynton in *Chagall*, (exhibition catalogue), Royal Academy of Arts, London, 1985, p. 21).

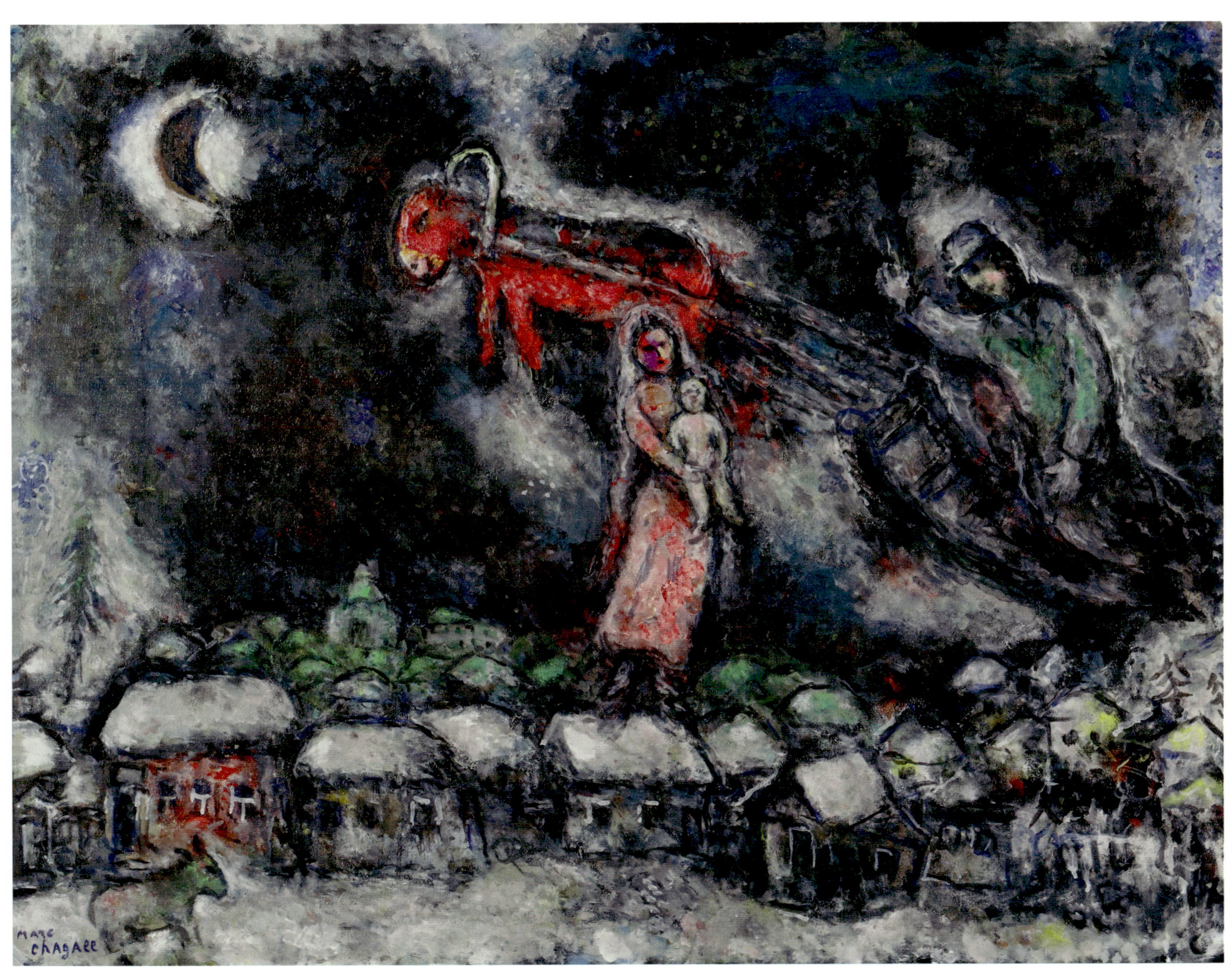

Marc
Chagall

Paysage de Paris
Executed in 1978
Oil, chinese ink, and colored crayons on masonite
13 × 16⅛ inches (33 × 41 cm)
Signed lower right: *Marc Chagall*
28031-002

PROVENANCE
Acquired by the present owner in 2006

This work is accompanied by a certificate of authenticity issued by the Comité Marc Chagall, signed by Jean-Louis Prat, dated Saint-Paul, 15th April 1996 (no. 96810).

This work is a study for one of Chagall's last major works, also entitled *Paysage de Paris*, one of the largest and most comprehensive paintings of the last years of Chagall's career. The larger work was painted over a seven year period and finally signed in 1978.

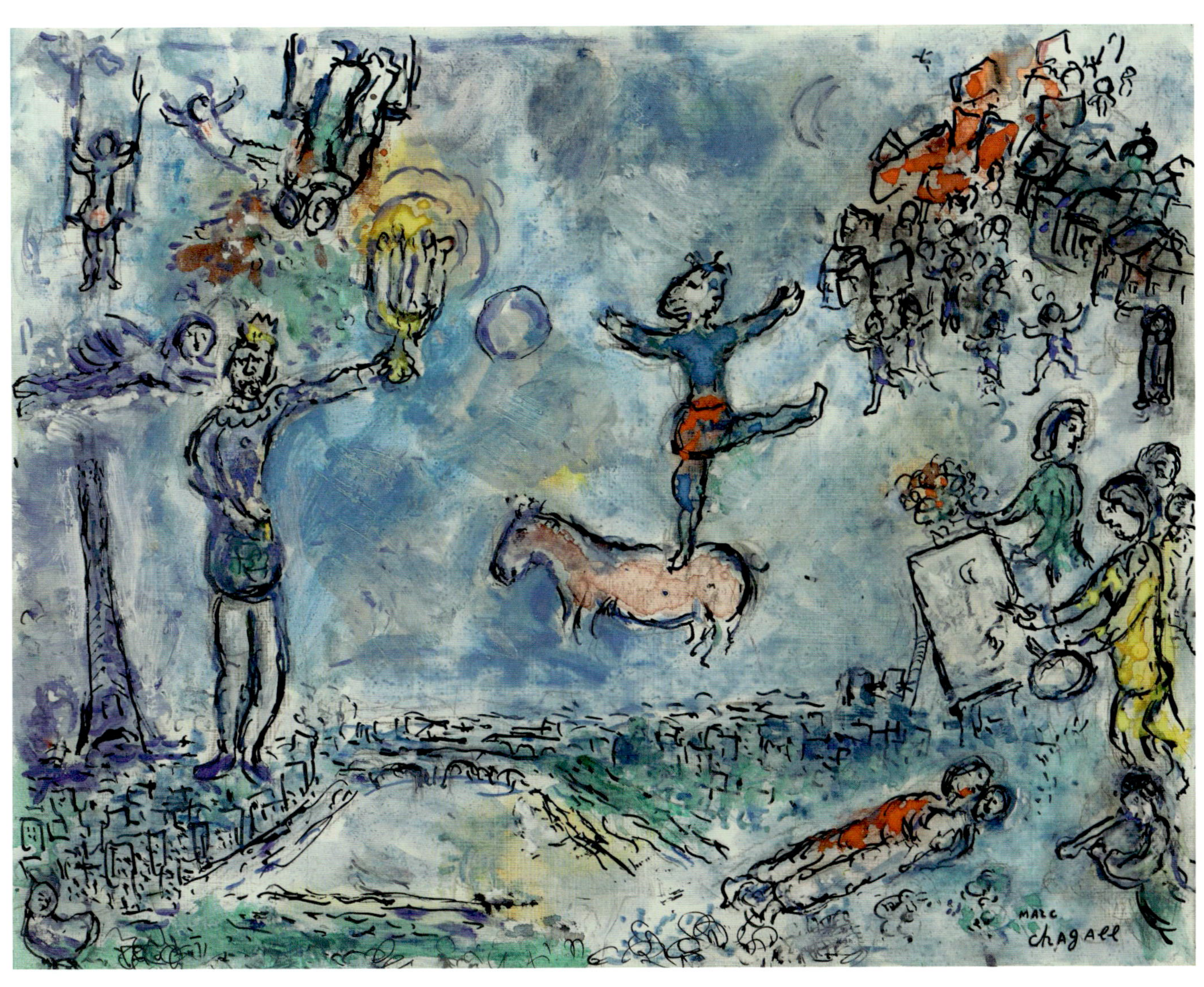

MARC CHAGALL

Devant la fenêtre à Saint-Paul
Executed in 1981
Tempera, pastel, and black ink on linen laid down on cardboard
13 × 18¹/₁₀ inches (33 × 46 cm)
Signed lower left by the artist in black India ink: *Chagall Marc*
28031-003

PROVENANCE
Acquired by the present owner in 2006

This work is accompanied by a certificate of authenticity issued by the Comité Marc Chagall, signed by Jean-Louis Prat and dated Paris, 3 April 2006 (no. 2006062).

Pairs of young lovers are featured throughout Chagall's oeuvre and are among the most important and symbolic of the cast of characters that appear in his paintings. "He is—he would surely wish one to say in summary—the painter of love, not just of the romantic love he portrays so often, nor of the love of parents and child, though these are not excluded, but of the wider, vastly more romantic love which embraces all mankind and all beings. 'In love lies the true Art: from it comes my technique, my religion; the new and old religion handed down to us from times long past'; and 'are not painting and colour inspired by Love? . . . In our life there is a single colour, as on an artist's palette, which provides the meaning of life and art. It is the color of love'" (as quoted in "Chagall 'over the Roofs of the World'" by Norbert Lynton in *Chagall*, (exhibition catalogue), Royal Academy of Arts, London, 1985, p. 20).

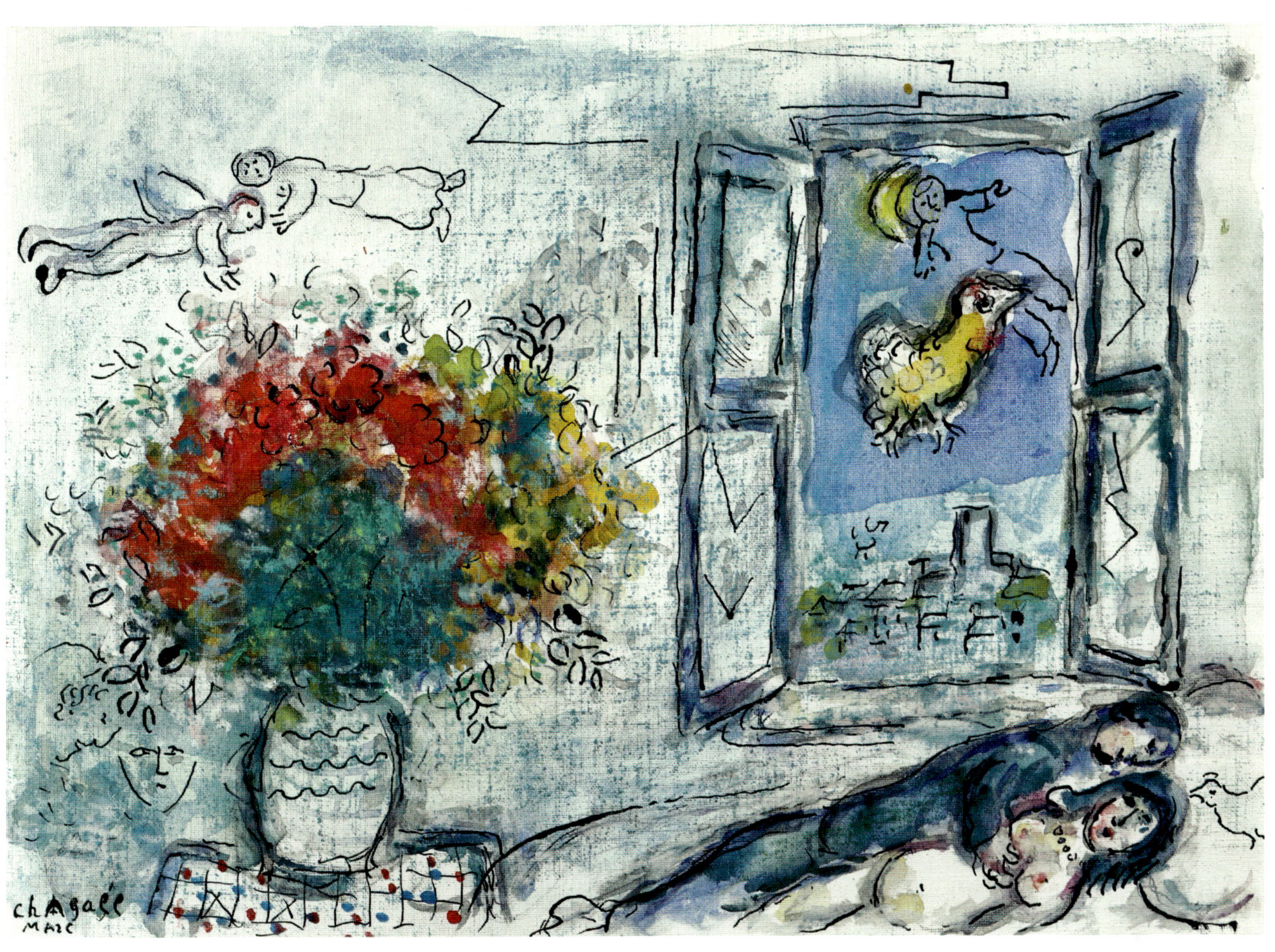

chagall
MArc

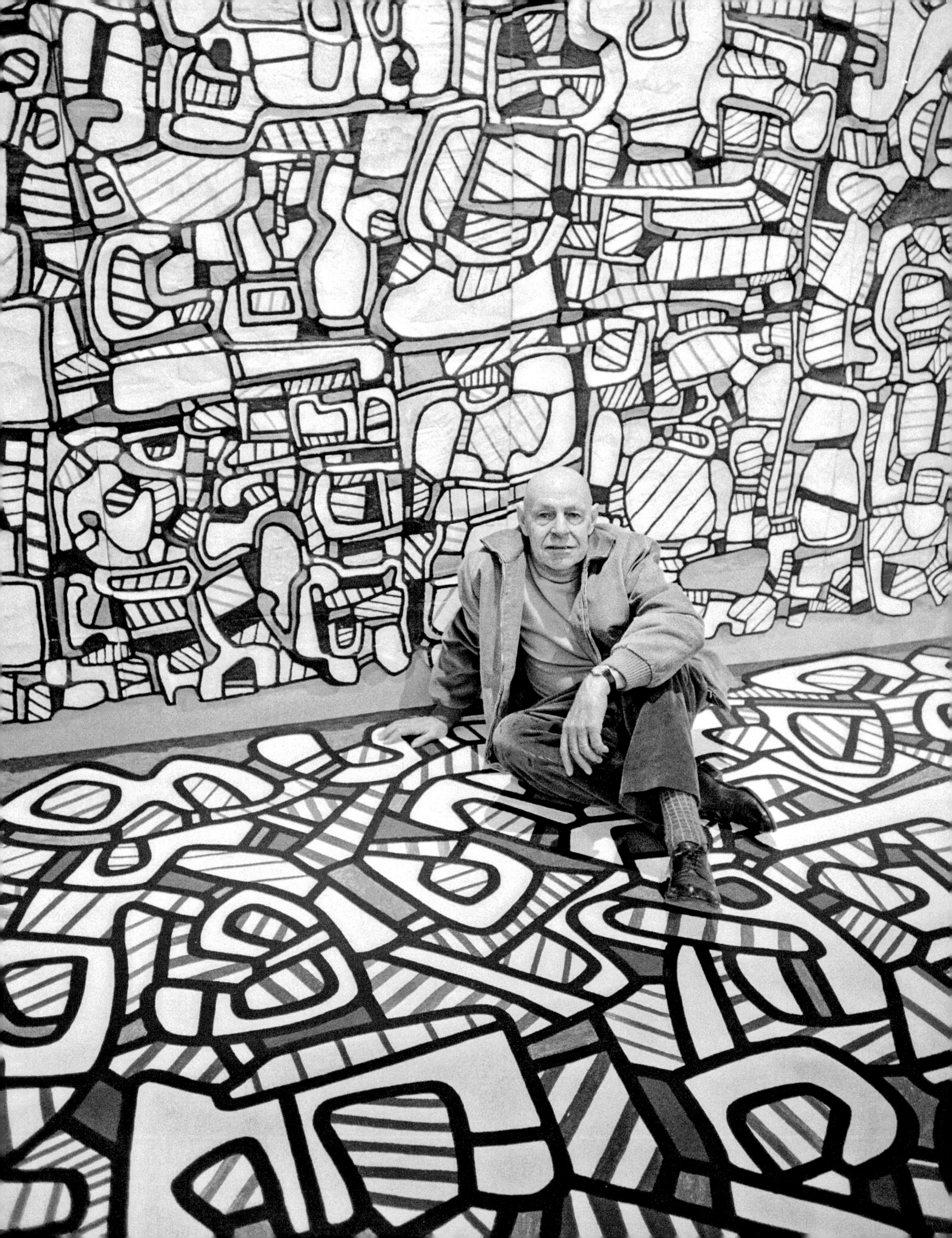

JEAN DUBUFFET (French, 1901–1985)

The immensely prolific Jean Dubuffet probably exercised a greater influence over both his European and his American contemporaries than any other artist of the immediate postwar epoch. He did this not only through his own work but also through his exploration and documentation of the phenomenon he named "Art Brut"—art produced by completely untrained artists, including children and psychotics, in which the artistic impulse seems to express itself in a completely "raw" state.

Dubuffet was born in Le Havre in 1901, the son of a prosperous wine merchant. As a young man, his ambition was to be an artist, but his first two attempts to establish himself in the art world were failures. He began studying to be a painter in Le Havre in 1916 and moved to Paris in 1918 to continue studying at the famous Académie Julien, but soon gave up, traveling first to Switzerland, then to Buenos Aires. In 1925, he returned home and entered the family wine business. This, after his father's death in 1927, became very prosperous under Dubuffet's direction. In 1933, after an interval of eight years, he began to paint again, but abandoned the effort four years later and returned to business.

In 1942 he rented a studio in Occupied Paris and returned to painting for a third time. His earliest mature works, created in the following year, were very simple and down to earth. They depicted, in a deliberately crude and childish style, people in the Metro and views of Paris in wartime. He had his first solo show in the heady atmosphere of newly-liberated Paris. The catalog preface was written by Dubuffet's friend Jean Paulhan, editor of the prestigious clandestine review *Les Lettres Françaises* under the German Occupation. The exhibition sharply divided opinion because of the apparent brutality of handling in the paintings.

Dubuffet was soon to push this aspect much further, experimenting with what he called "Hautes Pâtes," which made use of surfaces built up of plaster, glue and putty. The two objects exhibited here, deliberately primitive representations of a chair and a table, demonstrate his extension of this technique into sculpture. They are related to Dubuffet's major "Hourloupe" series, which originally began with a series of doodles done with an ordinary ballpoint pen. Dubuffet moved from drawings to paintings, then to fully three-dimensional objects. His aim was, he said, "to enter into the images, to inhabit them. . . . One sees oneself inside them, totally surrounded by one's mental productions."

In addition to working tirelessly on his own creations, Dubuffet became a very active promoter of Art Brut in all its forms, creating a permanent organization, the Compagnie de l'Art Brut, to collect and study such material. He declared: "There are (there are everywhere and always) two different orders of art. There is the art everyone is used to—polished or perfect art, baptized according to the moment either classic art, or romantic art (or whatever else one likes—it always comes to the same thing). And there is also, untamed and furtive, as some wild creature, Art Brut."

Jean Dubuffet in his highly decorated workshop at Cartoucherie de Vincennes, surrounded by works for the *Coucou Bazar*.

Guéridon (table) and Chaise de Pratique Fonction II (chair)

Guéridon (table)
Executed in 1972
Epoxy paint on polyurethane
26 × 22½ × 19¾ inches (66 × 57.2 cm)
Initialed and dated: *J.D. 72*

Chaise de Pratique Fonction II (chair)
Executed in 1969 and repainted by the artist in 1972
Polyester paint on polyurethane
41½ × 17 × 19 inches (105.4 × 43.2 × 48.3 cm)
Initialed and dated: *J.D. 72*

28026-006

PROVENANCE
The Pace Gallery, New York
Private collection, New York, 1974–2006
Acquired by the present owner in 2006

LITERATURE
Max Loreau, ed., *Catalogue des Travaux de Jean Dubuffet, Fascicule XXV: Arbres, Murs, Architectures*, cat. no. 163, p. 143, illustrated (Gueridon).
Max Loreau, ed., *Catalogue des Travaux de Jean Dubuffet, Fascicule XXIV: Tour aux Figures, Amoncellements, Cabinet Logologique*, cat. no. 137, p. 135, illustrated (Chaise de Pratique Fonction II).

Regarding Jean Dubuffet's 'Hourloupe Cycle' Mildred Glimcher, in her superb essay *Jean Dubuffet: Towards an alternative reality*, has explained:
"Within the Hourloupe Cycle, Dubuffet created an alternative world that encompassed all facets of the visual arts: drawing, painting, printmaking, sculpture, architecture and finally movement and music in the spectacle he called *Coucou Bazar*. The use of assemblage remained an essential constructional device in all aspects of these works. The Hourloupe *écriture*, or script that was the basic element of this alternative vision was not a transcription of reality but rather a product of his imagination. He described it as . . . 'a meandering, uninterrupted and resolutely uniform line, which brings all planes to the surface and takes no account of the concrete quality of the object described. . . . Thus this constantly uniform line, applied to all things (and, I insist not only to the things we see but also to those which have no concrete being . . .) reduces them to a common denominator and restores to us a continuous undifferentiated universe.'. . . In 1966, Dubuffet began to produce three-dimensional objects informed by the Hourloupe script. Dubuffet constructed the works from polystyrene, a lightweight white synthetic material that the artist could easily cut with a hot wire. He painted objects with the same flat contours and colors that characterized the patterned surfaces of the Hourloupe works. Dubuffet insisted that the new body of work represented three dimensional drawings and paintings, rather than sculpture in the traditional sense. As he stated: 'They do not belong to the realm of sculpture, but, rather, to that of painting, . . . which in this instance, has been, . . . endowed with a body, that is, corporalized, objectivated painting'" (as quoted in *Jean Dubuffet: Towards an Alternative Reality*, New York: Pace Publications, Inc., 1987, pp. 15–16).

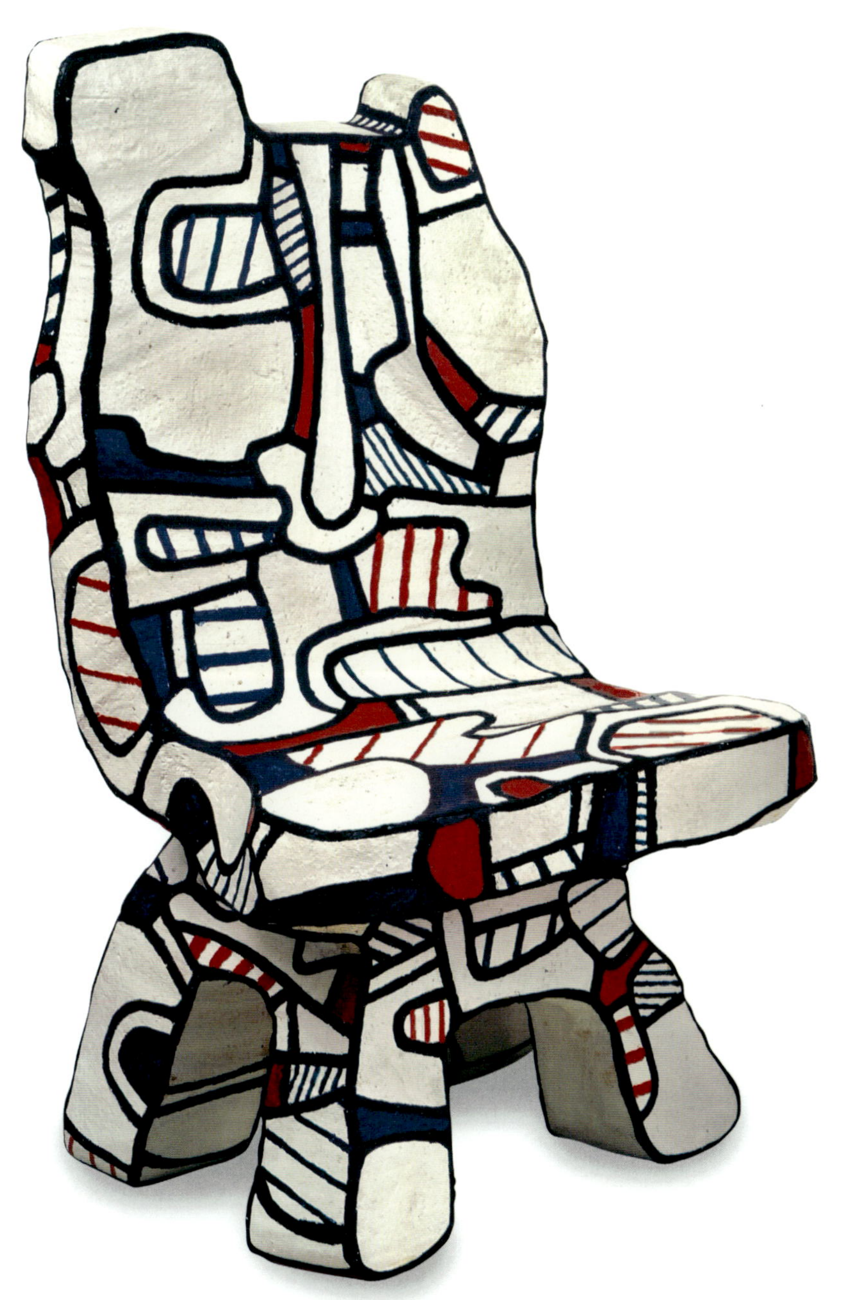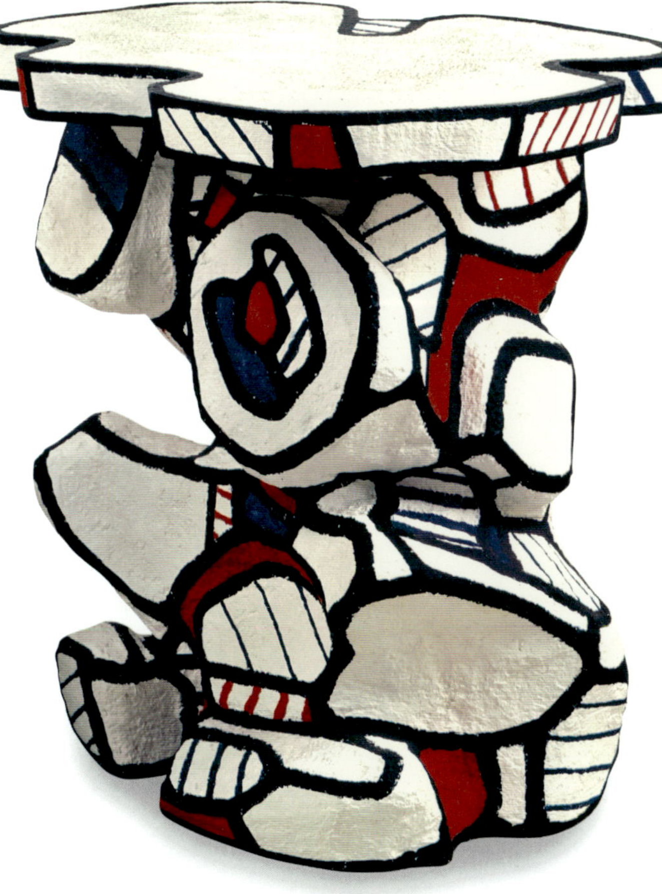

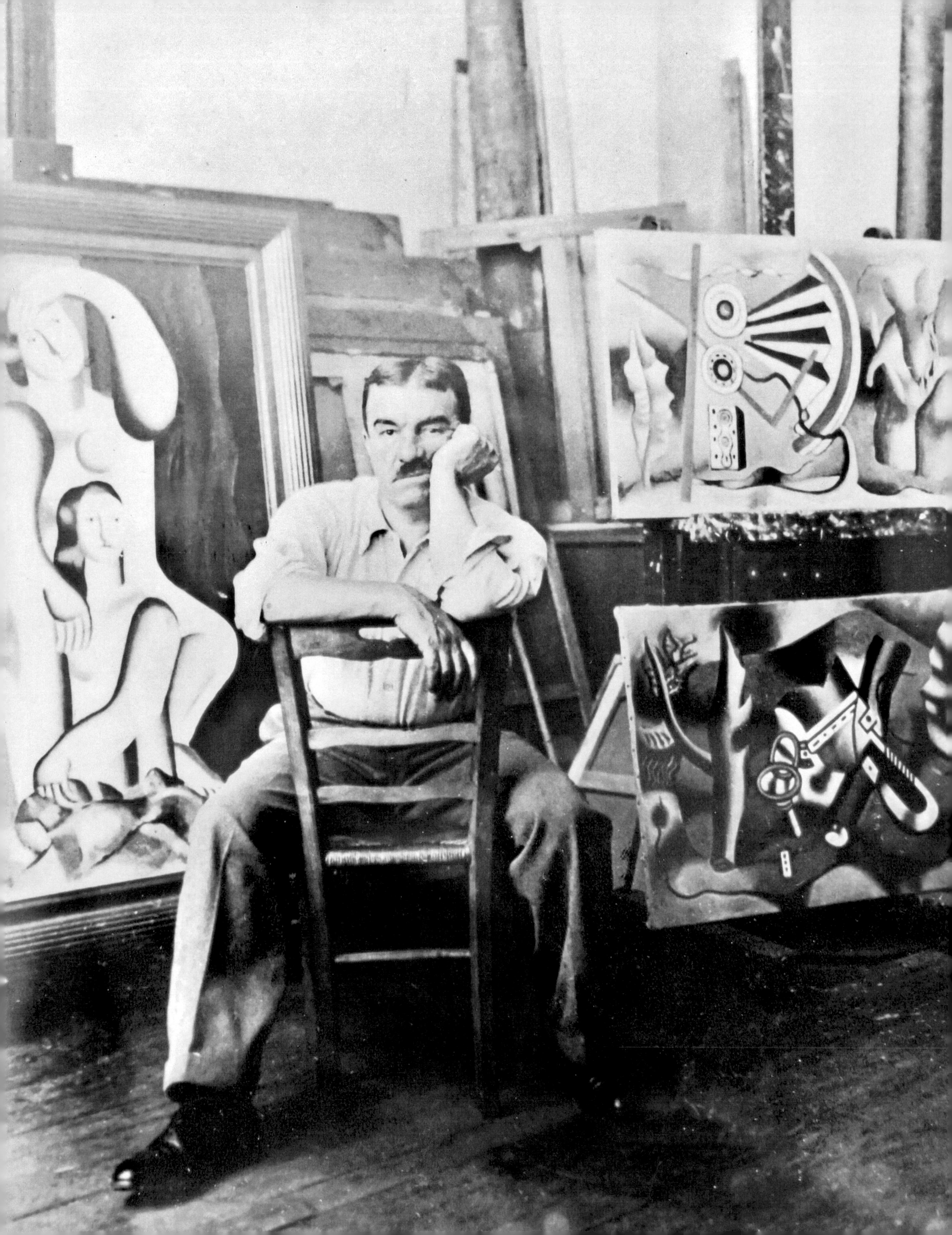

FERNAND LÉGER   (French, 1881–1955)

Léger was a relatively slow starter in the art world. He was born at Argentan in Normandy, and studied first at a school of architecture in Caen. He arrived in Paris in 1890, did jobbing work as an architectural draftsman and photographic retoucher, but found it hard to make any progress as a painter. A turning point for him was the great Cézanne retrospective held in 1907, as part of the Salon d'Automne. Afterwards he complained that he "had to spend years getting rid of Cézanne's influence." He came into contact with the burgeoning Cubist movement, and in particular with Guillaume Apollinaire, the chief advocate of the Cubists, though the two men never really liked one another. A more important advocate was the dealer Daniel-Henri Kahnweiler, who exhibited Picasso and Braque. In 1912 Kahnweiler bought all the paintings in Léger's studio and gave him a solo show. The next year, he offered Léger a contract.

These promising developments were cut short by the outbreak of World War I. Léger was mobilized early—in August 1914—and served in the ranks until he was gassed at Verdun in September 1916, after which he spent more than a year in the hospital. Later he was to say: "The war was a major event for me. At the Front there was a hyper-poetic atmosphere which excited me greatly . . . the war brought me down to earth. . . . I left Paris when I was painting entirely abstract work . . . suddenly I was at the level of the whole French people."

Throughout his subsequent career, Léger sought to combine populist elements with avant-garde ones, derived from his experience of Cubism. Among the influences detectable in the works chosen for this exhibition are not only the ambitious neo-classical canvases of Jacques-Louis David, but also the popular prints called *imageries d'Épinal*, which derive their name from the town of Épinal in the Vosges, where they were produced in large quantities in the 19th and early 20th centuries. The prints cover subjects of all kinds—political, religious and satirical.

During World War II, Léger moved to the United States, where he already had strong connections. While in America, he taught at Yale and at Mills College in Oakland, California, and exhibited his work at the Fogg Art Museum. Though he returned to France in December 1945—that is to say, as soon as return was possible—he must be regarded as being part of the story of American, as well as of French 20th century art. In particular, he is very obviously an ancestor of the American Pop Art of the 1960s, though this is little mentioned in the standard histories of the Pop Movement.

The works exhibited here, dating from the inter-war years, show Léger as a fully mature artist. They demonstrate his innate classicism and his powerful sense of the decorative.

Fernand Léger in his studio,
1933. Photograph by Galatine

FERNAND LÉGER

Composition d'objets
Painted in 1929
Oil on canvas
36¼ × 28¾ inches (92 × 73 cm)
Signed and dated lower left: *F. LÉGER/29*
Enverso titled, signed, and dated: *Composition d'objets, F. LEGER '29*
28031-008

PROVENANCE
Mme. Fernand Léger, Paris
Galerie Louise Leiris, Paris (Inv. no. 08257/30164)
Acquired by the present owner in 1990

EXHIBITED
Lyon, Musée des Beaux-Arts, *Fernand Léger*, 1955, no. 42.
Basel, Kunsthalle, *Fernand Léger*, 1957, no. 56.
Munich, Haus der Kunst, *Fernand Léger 1881–1955*, 1957, no. 57.
Zurich, Kunsthaus, *Fernand Léger*, 1957, no. 72.
Colmar, Musée d'Unterlinden, *Fernand Léger 1881–1855*, 1966, no.3.
Geneva, Galerie Motte, 1974.
Paris, Galerie 22, *F. Léger*, 1974, no. 11, illustrated p. 17.
Geneva, Musée de l'Athénée, *Léger, Vasarely*, 1979, no. 11, illustrated.

LITERATURE
Georges Bauquier, *Fernand Léger. Le catalogue raisonné de l'oeuvre peint (1929–31)*, vol. IV,
    Paris, 1993, p. 38, no. 618, p. 39, illustrated in color.

Regarding Léger's work of the late 1920s, Gaston Diehl has written "At this point, a fresh
wind blew through his work and enlivened it, sweeping into the past the omnipresent
sterility of the machine and gradually bringing about drastic changes in his art. . . . For
he had the idea, which one may well call inspired and was undoubtedly suggested by
films or the stage, to implement a new concept of space: he introduced into his paintings
indeterminate and boundless space. This freely enabled him to draw symbols or figures
in a fantastic ballet whose appearance, even though it was based on reality, was no longer
subject to earthly laws and could, if he so desired, be raised to the level of a truly poetic
creation, total and absolute in its lyricism. . . . With his familiar irony, which should not be
misinterpreted, the artist commented on the decision that led him to this period of "objects
in space": 'I took an object, I did away with the table, I put the table in the air, without
support and without perspective.' He previously explained: 'I have scattered objects in
space and have connected them with one another while causing them to radiate from the
foreground of the painting. This is a simple game of rhythm and harmony made up of
primary colors and planes, conducting lines, distances and contrasts" (*Fernand Léger*,
New York, 1985, p. 39).

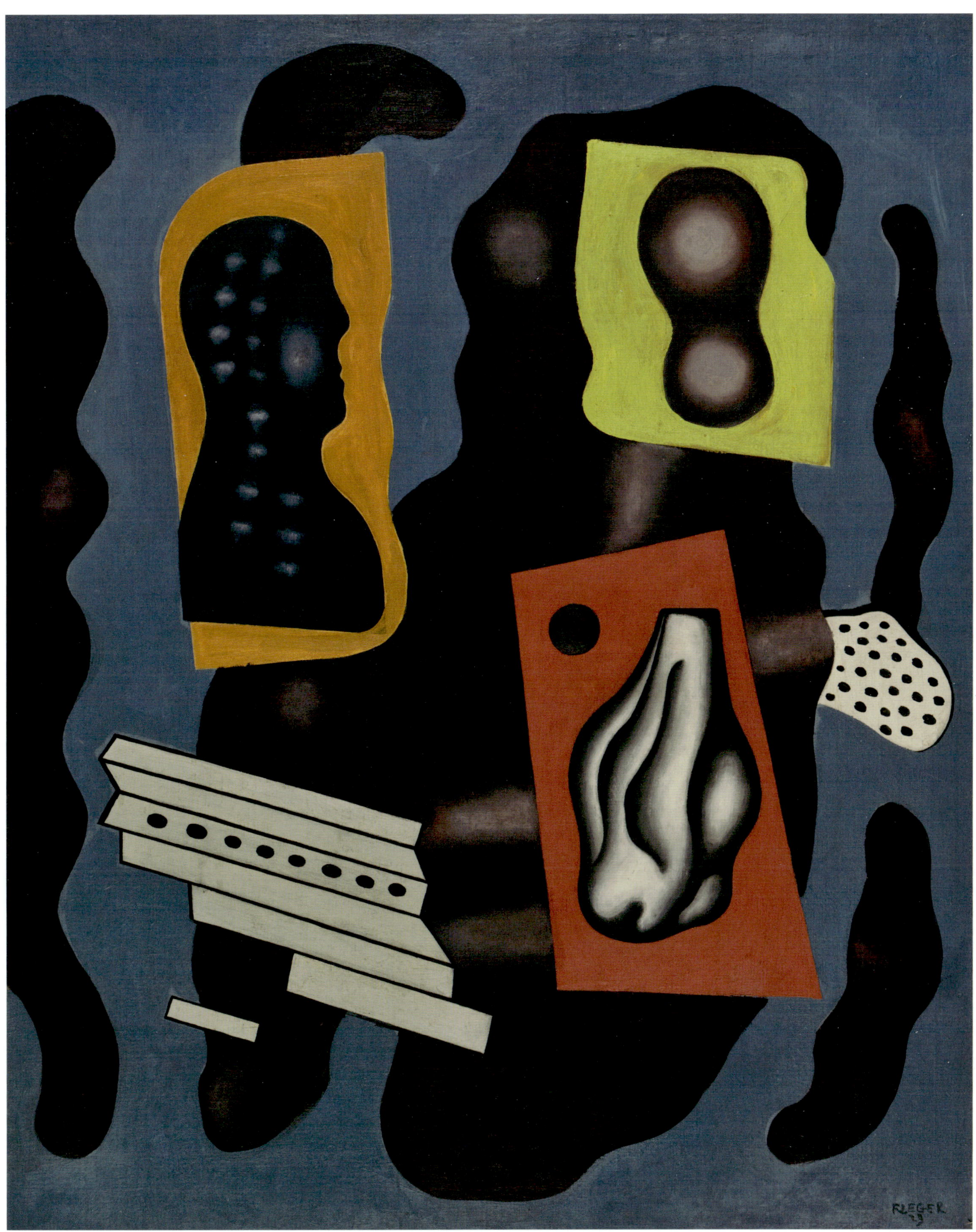

FERNAND LÉGER

La Danseuse
Painted in 1929
Oil on canvas
25³/₄ × 21¹/₂ inches (65 × 55 cm)
Signed and dated lower right: *F.LÉGER 29*
28005-003

PROVENANCE
Perls Galleries, New York
Daniel Malingue, Paris
Private collection
Perls Galleries, New York
Private collection
Acquired by the present owner circa 2003

EXHIBITED
New York, Perls Galleries, *Fernand Léger*, 1952, no. 11.
New York, Perls Galleries, *French Modern Paintings*, 1953, no. 72.
New York, Perls Galleries, *Modern French Paintings*, 1954, no. 98.
New York, Perls Galleries, *Fernand Léger*, 1955, no. 11.
New York, Perls Galleries, *Fernand Léger: Oil Paintings*, 1968, no. 7.
Paris, Galerie Berggruen, *Fernand Léger*, 1975, no. 21, illustrated.
New York, Hammer Galleries, *19th and 20th Century Paintings: Recent Acquisitions*, 1991,
    p. 26, illustrated.

LITERATURE
Georges Bauquier, *Fernand Léger, Catalogue raisonné de l'oeuvre peint (1929–31)*, volume IV,
    Paris, 1994, no. 649.

"Léger's work and own thinking was clearly in transition in the late 1920s and early 1930s.
The work produced during this period is perhaps among the most enigmatic, iconographically-
speaking, of his career. But it acts as a kind of bridge between the machine aesthetic of the
immediate postwar period, and the monumental figurative work of the late 1930s onward,
allowing those two aspects of his career to come full circle in effect. The close-up, the
fragment, the object, and the objective as rethought, reworked and reshuffled during these
years, become the basis for Léger's enduring world view that allows renewed realism to
re-enter what had previously been a relatively abstract art" (Judi Freeman, "L'Evénement
d'Objectivité Plastique: Léger's Shift From the Mechanical to the Figurative, 1926–1933," in
the catalogue *Fernand Léger: The Later Years*, Whitechapel Art Gallery, London, 1987, p. 31).

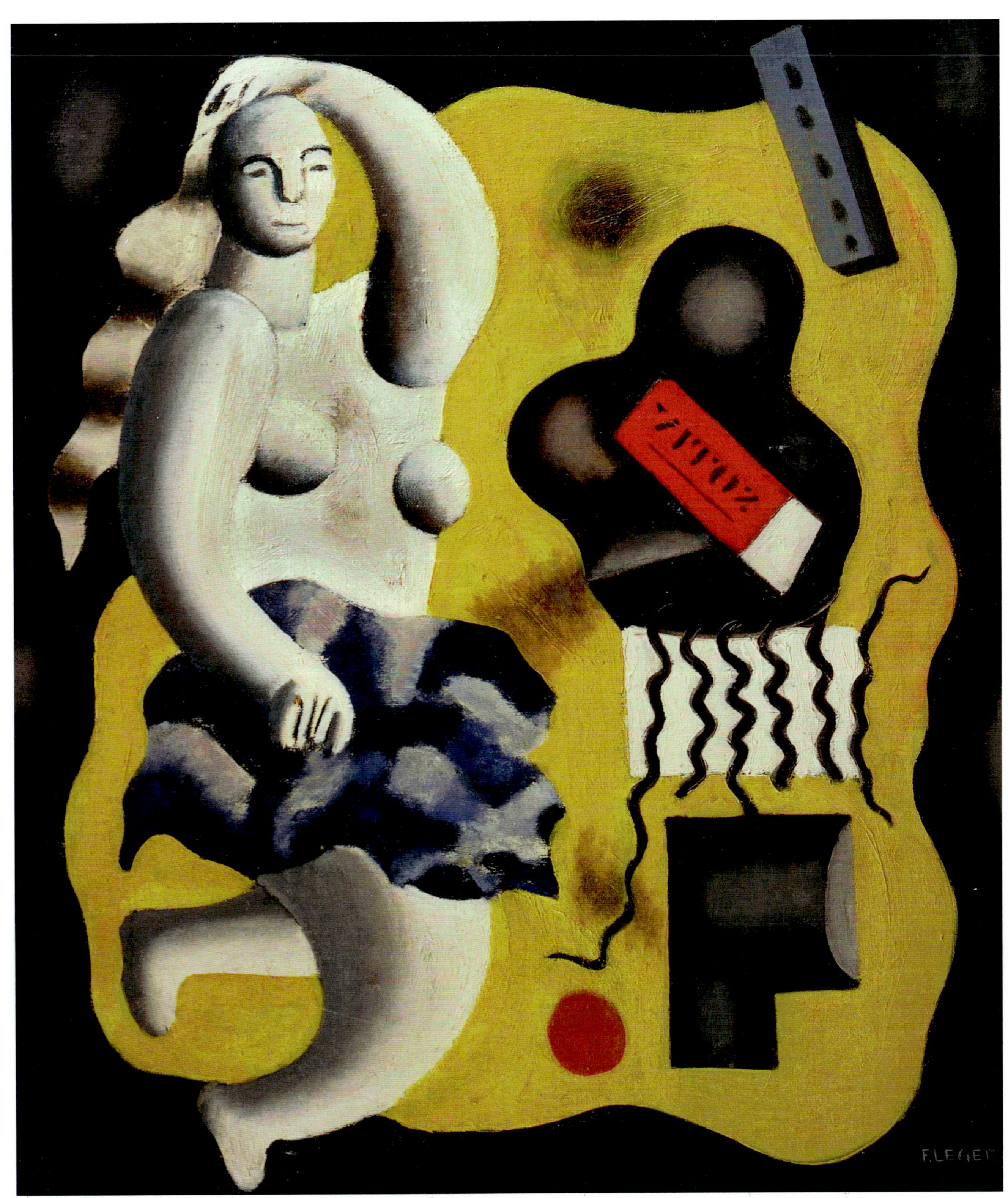
ZULU
F.LEGER

Composition au buste
Executed in 1938
Gouache and pencil on paper
15¾ × 20⅛ inches (40 × 51 cm)
Initialed and dated: *FL '38*
28031-009

PROVENANCE
Galerie Louise Leiris, Paris (Inv. no. 02167/30149)
Acquired by the present owner in 1989

This work is accompanied by a photo-certificate issued by the Galerie Louise Leiris, signed by Maurice Jardot and dated Paris, 20 June 1985.

The large "polychrome flower" appears in many of Leger's works of the thirties. As Werner Schmalenbach explains: "During the thirties Léger painted a great many still lifes. They reveal the same change in style as his large compositions—free-floating forms, often abstract or floral; plantlike instead of geometric forms, which become increasingly rare. It is significant that Léger busied himself just then more intensively with drawings from nature: leaves, roots, and tree trunks. Plant life, which first appeared with a new freedom in *Woman Bathing* of 1931 assumes an importance in his work that his 'Mechanical Period' would hardly have led one to expect" (*Léger*, New York, 1985, pp. 34–35).

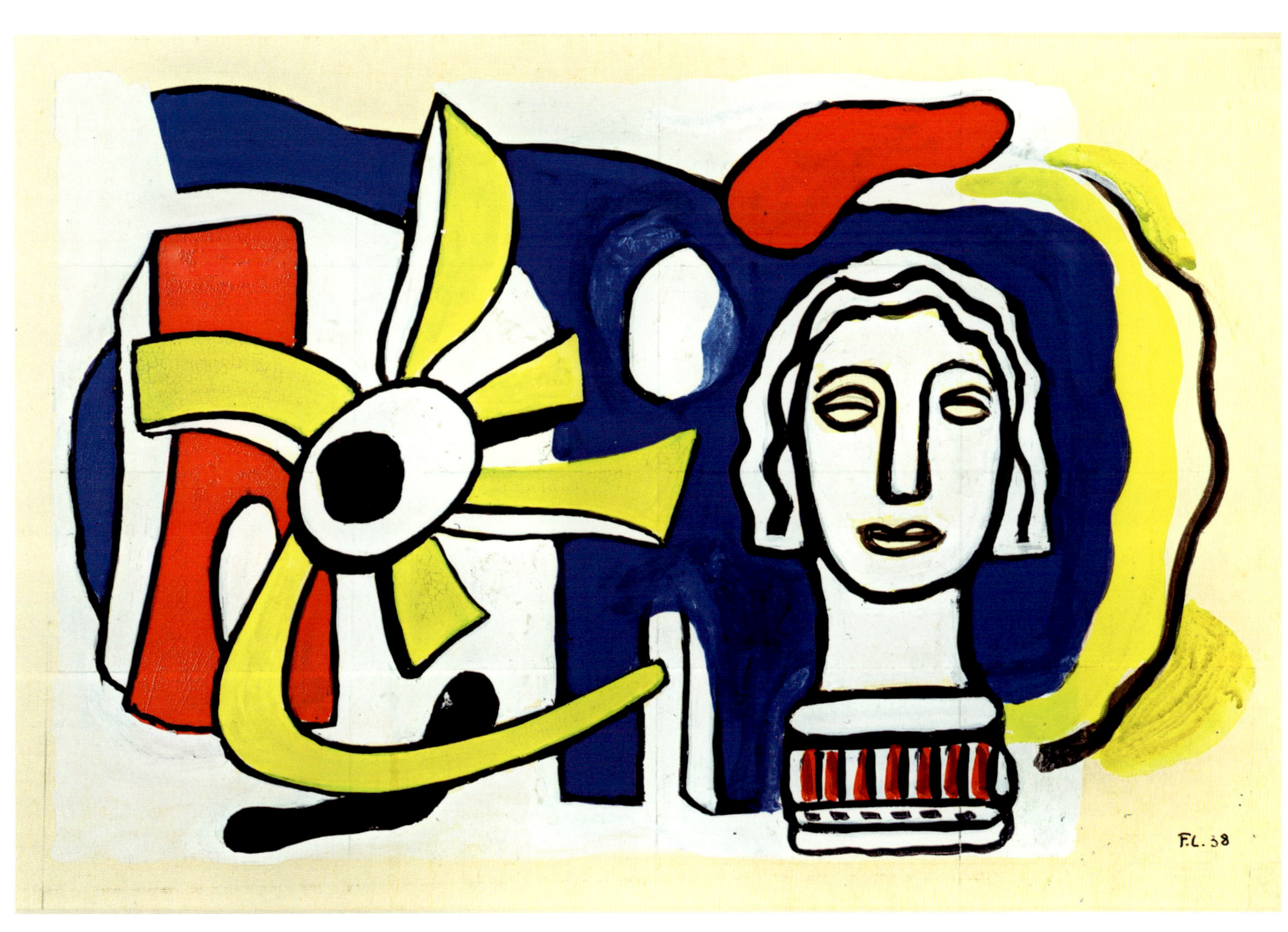

Composition aux trois profils
Painted in 1937
Oil on canvas
35 × 51¼ inches (89 × 130 cm)
Signed and dated lower right: *F. Léger. 37*
28017-002

PROVENANCE
Galerie Simon, Paris
Galerie Louise Leiris, Paris (Inv. 0766/6614)
Acquired by the present owner in 1999

EXHIBITED
Prague, Galerie S V, *Pariz 1938*, 1938, no. 32.
Stockholm, Svesk-Franska Konstgalleriet, *Peintres de Paris*, 1946, no. 97.
Bern, Kunsthalle, *Fernand Léger*, 1952, no. 67.
London, Marlborough Fine Art Ltd., *Fernand Léger, paintings, drawings, lithographs,
    ceramics*, 1954–55, no. 18.
Liège, Musée de l'Art Wallon, *Léger, Matisse, Picasso, Miró, Laurens, Magnelli, Arp, Hartung,
    Jacobsen*, 1958, no. 15, illustrated.
Paris, Galerie Louise Leiris, *Fernand Léger, 55 œuvres, 1913–1953*, 1985, no. 39, p. 47, illustrated.

LITERATURE
Fernand Léger, *Fonctions de la peinture*, 1965, Paris, Editions Gonthier, Bibliotheque
    Mediations, illustrated.
Serge Fauchereau, *Fernand Léger*, New York: Rizzoli, 1994, no. 90.
Georges Bauquier, *Fernand Léger, Le catalogue raisonne de l'oeuvre peint*, (1932–1937), vol. V,
    1996, p. 278, no. 965, p. 279, illustrated.

"The human body is of no weightier plastic interest than a tree, a plant, a piece of rock, or
a pile of rope. It is enough to compose a picture with these objects, being careful to chose
those that may best create a composition . . . There is neither an abstract picture nor a
concrete one. There is a beautiful picture and a bad picture. There is the picture that moves
you and the one that leaves you indifferent . . . If I isolate a tree in a landscape, if I approach
that tree, I see that its bark has an interesting design and a plastic form; that its branches
have dynamic violence which ought to be observed; that its leaves are decorative. Locked up
in 'subject matter,' these elements are not 'set in value.' It is here that the 'new realism' finds
itself" (Fernand Léger, "The New Realism Goes On," 1936, quoted in Carolyn Lanchner,
Fernand Leger, (exhibition catalogue), Museum of Modern Art, New York, 1998, p. 139).

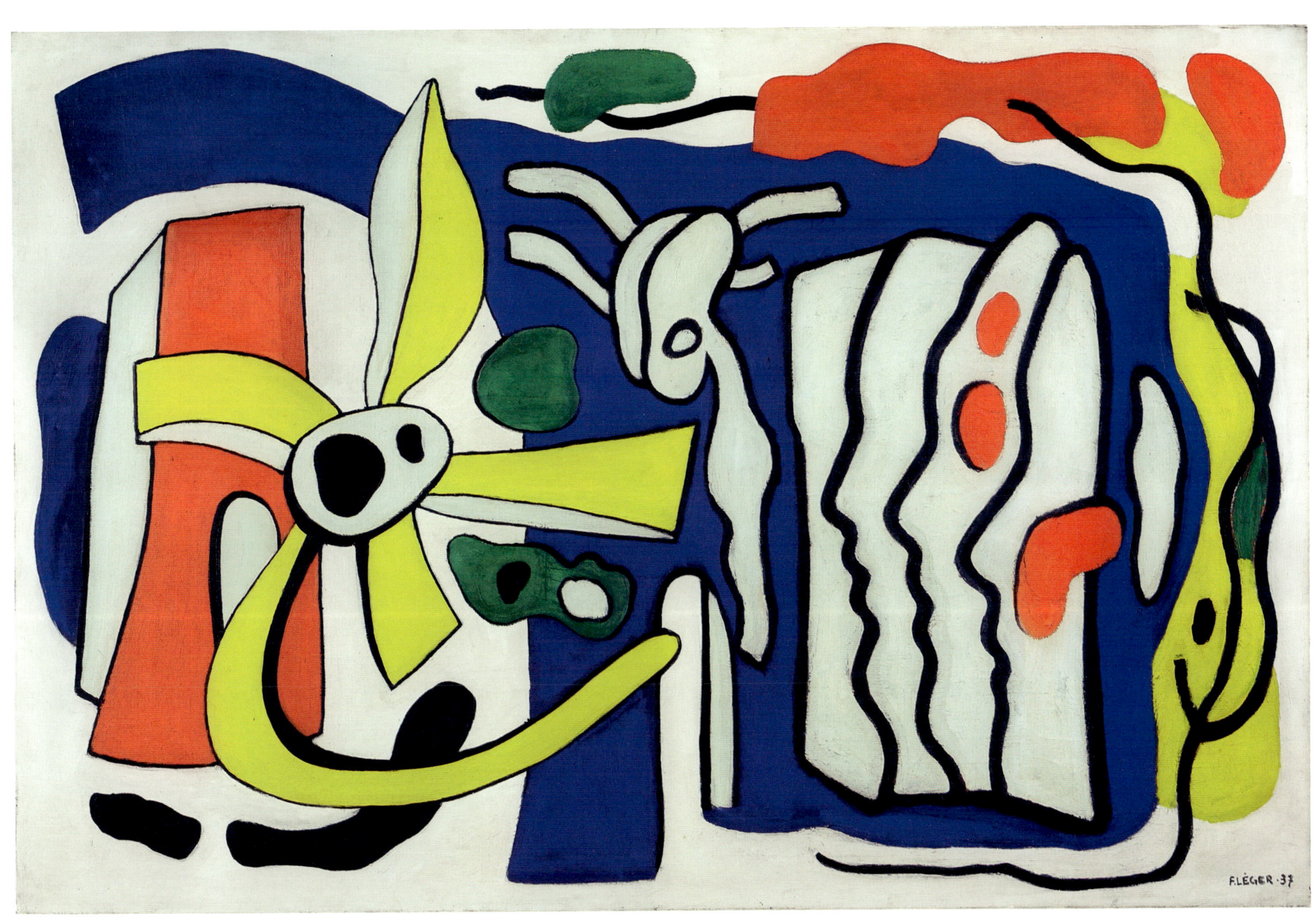
F.LÉGER·37

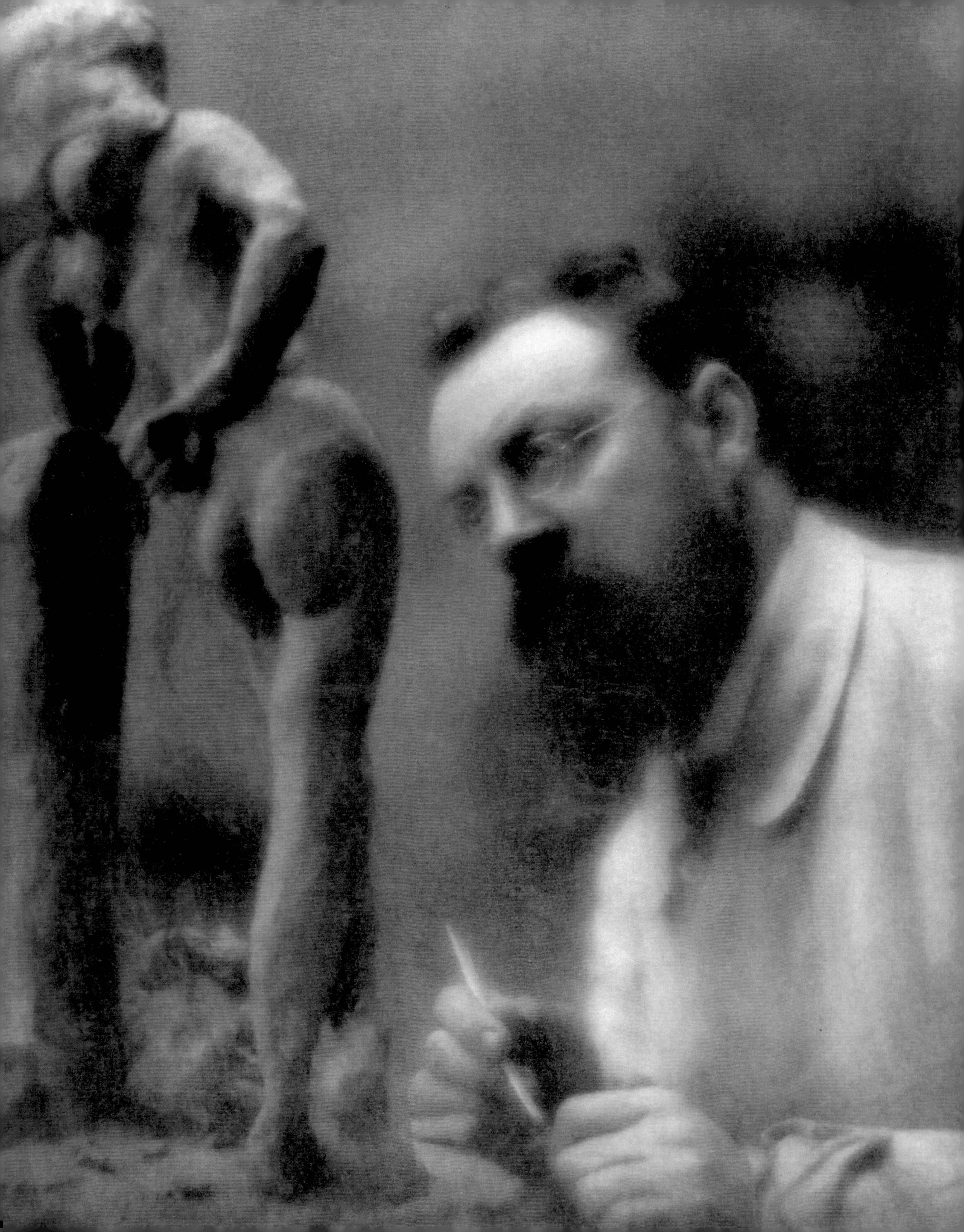

HENRI MATISSE (French, 1869–1954)

After a slow beginning—he was the son of a grain merchant who did not approve of his son's ambition to become a painter—Matisse was, after fifteen years of struggle, established as the leader of the Paris avant-garde through the triumph enjoyed both by himself and his followers at the Salon d'Automne of 1905. The new painters who then burst upon the scene were nicknamed the 'Fauves' or 'wild beasts' by critics who were half-indignant, half-thrilled by the coloristic daring of their work. Matisse was "the king of the Fauves"— the biggest lion in the jungle.

Soon after this, he jotted down some 'Notes of a Painter' for *La Grande Revue*, an important Parisian periodical. The article was published at the end of 1908. For a "Lion King," its tone is surprisingly pacific: "What I am after above all is expression. . . . Expression to my way of thinking does not consist of the passion mirrored upon a human face or betrayed by a violent gesture. The whole arrangement of my pictures is expressive. . . . Composition is the art of arranging in a decorative manner the various elements at a painter's disposal for the expression of his feelings."

Basically he was to stick to this credo for the whole of the rest of his career.

If the Salon d'Automne was the first turning point in Matisse's career, the second was World War I. When the war broke out, he was already over military age. He struggled for two years with the cold and privations of wartime Paris, then retired to Nice. What was at first a temporary arrangement soon became permanent. Nice became Matisse's base for the rest of his life. There he gradually evolved a way of life devoted to painting. He was perhaps encouraged in this by visits he made to Renoir, by that time crippled with arthritis and coming to the end of his long life.

The painting exhibited here, *Intérieur—porte overte*, painted circa 1920–21, perfectly encapsulates the atmosphere that Matisse created around himself as a fully mature artist. The sculptures belong to a slightly earlier epoch. One of the interesting things about the major artists of the École de Paris, Picasso as well as Matisse, is that, having begun their careers as painters, they then moved into sculpture as they matured, bringing with them a creative disrespect for established sculptural traditions.

The beautiful late drawing of a woman's head demonstrates two apparently contradictory elements in Matisse's art. First, that he was a master of simplification. Second, that he was a sharp observer of human character. Matisse loved women for their characters, perhaps indeed because they offered a mystery he never completely solved.

Henri Matisse sculpting a clay nude, circa January 1915. Photograph by Edward Steichen

Petit nu accroupi avec bras
Conceived in 1908 and cast in 1952 in an edition of 11
Bronze
5⅝ × 3½ × 4 inches (14.4 × 9 × 10 cm)
Marked with initials: *HM*; numbered: *9*
Stamped: *C. Valsuani cire perdue*
28026-008

PROVENANCE
Pierre Matisse Gallery, New York
Mrs. Victor Leventritt, New York
Acquired by the present owner in 2005

EXHIBITIONS
Institut Valencia d'Art Modern, *Henri Matisse*, October 21, 2003– January 11, 2004, p. 169,
   illustrated.

LITERATURE
Matisse Archive No. 135 (formerly 221).
Albert E. Elsen, *The Sculpture of Henri Matisse*, New York: Harry N. Abrams, 1972, p. 100
   (illustration of another cast).
Isabelle Monod-Fontaine, *The Sculpture of Henri Matisse*, London: Thames and Hudson,
   1984, no. 29 (illustration of another cast).
Claude Duthuit, *Matisse: Catalogue raisonné de l'oeuvre sculpté*, Paris, 1997, no. 37, p. 80
   (illustration of another cast).

Matisse frequently worked from photographs rather than live models when creating his
sculpted nudes, believing that his own translation of two dimensions into three allowed
him greater freedom to invent the form of the body. The photograph on which this
sculpture was based was reproduced in *Le Monde Photographique* (Claude Duthuit, *Matisse:
Catalogue raisonné de l'oeuvre sculpté*, Paris, 1997, p. 384, Note 16).

   As Matisse explained, his sculptures should be considered as a means of exploration:
"I took up sculpture because what interested me in painting was a clarification of my ideas.
I changed my method and worked in clay in order to have a rest from painting . . . by
changing the medium I do not change the goal. . . . I do not consider my sculpture anything
but an exercise (quoted in *Matisse: Painter as Sculptor*, (exhibition catalogue), Baltimore
Museum of Art, 2007, pp. 17–18).

   Matisse also commented: "In addition to the sensations one derives from a drawing, a
sculpture must invite us to handle it as an object; just so the sculptor must feel, in making
it, the particular demands for volume and mass. The smaller the bit of sculpture, the more
the essential of forms must exist" (Henri Matisse as quoted in Jack Flam (ed.), *Matisse on
Art*, Los Angeles: University of California Press, 1995, p. 5).

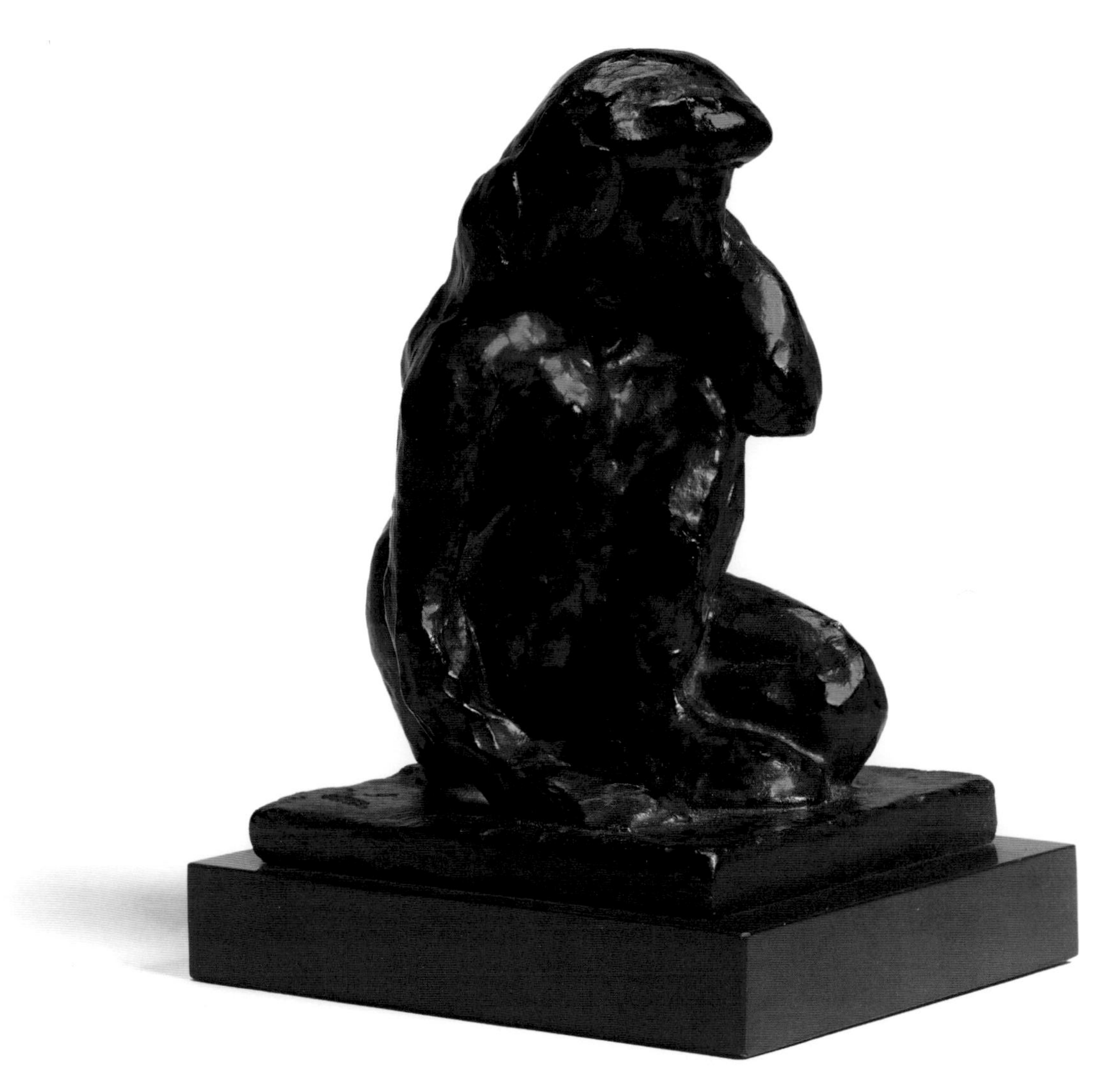

Nu couché au polochon
Conceived in Nice in 1918, cast circa 1930
Bronze with brown patina
$5\frac{1}{8} \times 10\frac{3}{8} \times 4\frac{1}{8}$ inches (13 × 26.2 × 10.5 cm)
Marked with initials: *HM*; and numbered: *7/10* on the side of the cushion
Stamped on corner: *C. Valsuani cire perdue*
28026-007

PROVENANCE
Galerie Samlaren, Stockholm
Private collection (circa 1952–1989)
Acquired by the present owner in 1989

LITERATURE
Albert E. Elsen, "The Sculpture of Matisse, Part II: Old Problems and New Possibilities,"
    Artforum, Oct. 1968.
Mario Luzi and Massimo Carra, *L'Opera di Matisse dalla rivolta 'Fauve'all'intimismo, 1904–1928*,
    Milan 1971, p. 109, no. S18, p. 108 (illustration of another cast).
Albert E. Elsen, *The Sculpture of Henri Matisse*, New York 1972, pp. 140, 143 and 144 (illustration
    of another cast).
Alfred H. Barr, *Matisse: His Art and His Public*, London 1975, p. 424 (illustration of another cast).
Michael P. Mezzatesta, *Henri Matisse Sculptor/Painter*, Fort Worth, Texas, 1984, pp. 110–112
    (illustration of another cast).
Isabelle Monod-Fontaine, *The Sculpture of Henri Matisse*, London, 1984, no. 54, p. 147
    (illustration of another cast).
Pierre Schneider, *Matisse*, New York, 1984, p. 552 (illustration of another cast).
Claude Duthuit, *Matisse: Catalogue raisonné de l'oeuvre sculpté*, Paris, 1997, pp. 175 & 177
    (illustration of another cast).

Matisse spent the winter of 1917–18 in Nice and returned in November of 1918. It is during this
period that he began working at the École des Arts Decoratifs modeling from plaster casts of
ancient and Renaissance sculpture. It is possible that these sculptures, specifically an antique
crouching Venus type in Nice or the Louvre's *Crouching Venus* marble, inspired his work. The
suggestion that the bolster (polochon) on which the figure in this sculpture leans comes from
Matisse's hotel room provides evidence for the work being executed in Nice.
     Albert E. Elsen supposed that *Petit nu au polochon* represented the final stage of a three step
process coming after Matisse's Venus figures: "the first *(Nu accroupi)*, the continued flow of
ideas, masculine energy, and recklessness from the paintings; then a return *(Venus accroupi)* to
the patience, discipline and pleasure of studying museum art; and finally *(Petit nu au polochon)*
a new mood of contentment and détente in his style." Elsen further noted that in the present
sculpture "there is a lessening of the tension and disciplined reworking of its predecessors.
The woman sprawls luxuriously, her form loose and free of any circumscribing geometry. The
feeling of détente in this last sculpture complements what was happening in the paintings,
where for many years Matisse was to avoid tautness of drawing and to lighten his touch and
palette" (*The Sculpture of Henri Matisse*, New York, 1972, pp. 141, 143–144).

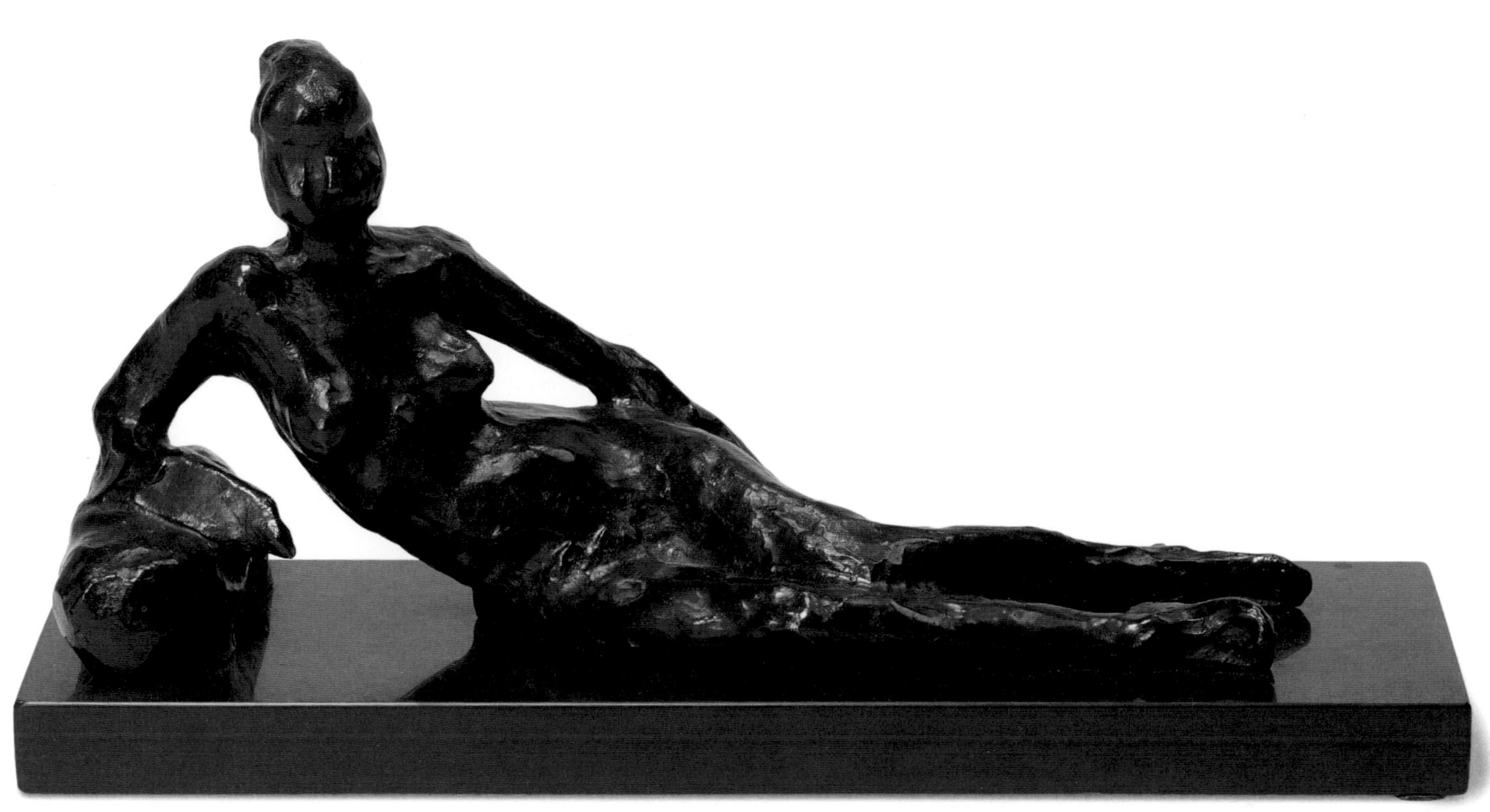

HENRI MATISSE

Intérieur—porte ouverte
Painted circa 1920–21
Oil on canvas
15 × 18⅛ inches (38.1 × 46 cm)
Signed lower right: *Henri.Matisse*
28005-008

PROVENANCE
Bernheim-Jeune, Paris, 1924 (no. 4972)
Henri Canonne, Paris, 1924
The Lefevre Gallery (Alex Reid & Lefevre, Ltd.), London, 1930
M. Knoedler & Company, Inc., Paris, New York, London, 1951
Private collection, Europe (acquired in the 1960's and with the same family until 2008)
Acquired by the present owner in 2008

EXHIBITION
Paris, Galerie Bernheim Jeune, *Henri Matisse*, May 1924, (probably) no. 37.

LITERATURE
Pierre Courthion, *Henri Matisse*, Paris, 1934, pl. 38, illustrated.
Guy-Patrice & Michel Dauberville, *Matisse*, vol. II, Paris, 1995, no. 428, p. 934, illustrated
     p. 935.

This work is accompanied by a photo-certificate of authenticity dated Paris 5/1/2009 from
Mme. Wanda de Guébriant stating the piece is numbered PW46 in the archives of the artist.

Matisse painted *Intérieur—porte ouverte* circa 1920–21, during a pivotal moment in his career,
when he was spending more and more time in the South of France, but continuing to head
to Paris and his native North on a regular basis. Here, through the door, there are levels of
foreground, sea and sky that allow for a variety of colors to fill the space, creating a picture-
within-a-picture, allowing a landscape into an interior and introducing a certain variety, a
visual counterpoint to the yellows of the walls. The window motif was one that Matisse had
explored again and again since his holiday with André Derain in Collioure in 1905.

Matisse conjures sensation, avoiding realism in favor of a subjective, lyrical capturing
of some of the emotional state, some of the feelings, felt by the artist at the time of painting.
"There was no question any longer of evoking memories of the sea, the countryside, etc.,"
Matisse explained, "What mattered now was making a construction. It was the vibration
of the individual that counted rather than the object that produced the emotion; what was
rendered was not material but the human emotion, a certain elevation of mind that could
spring from any sensation" (quoted in Pierre Schneider, *Matisse*, London, 1984, p. 85).

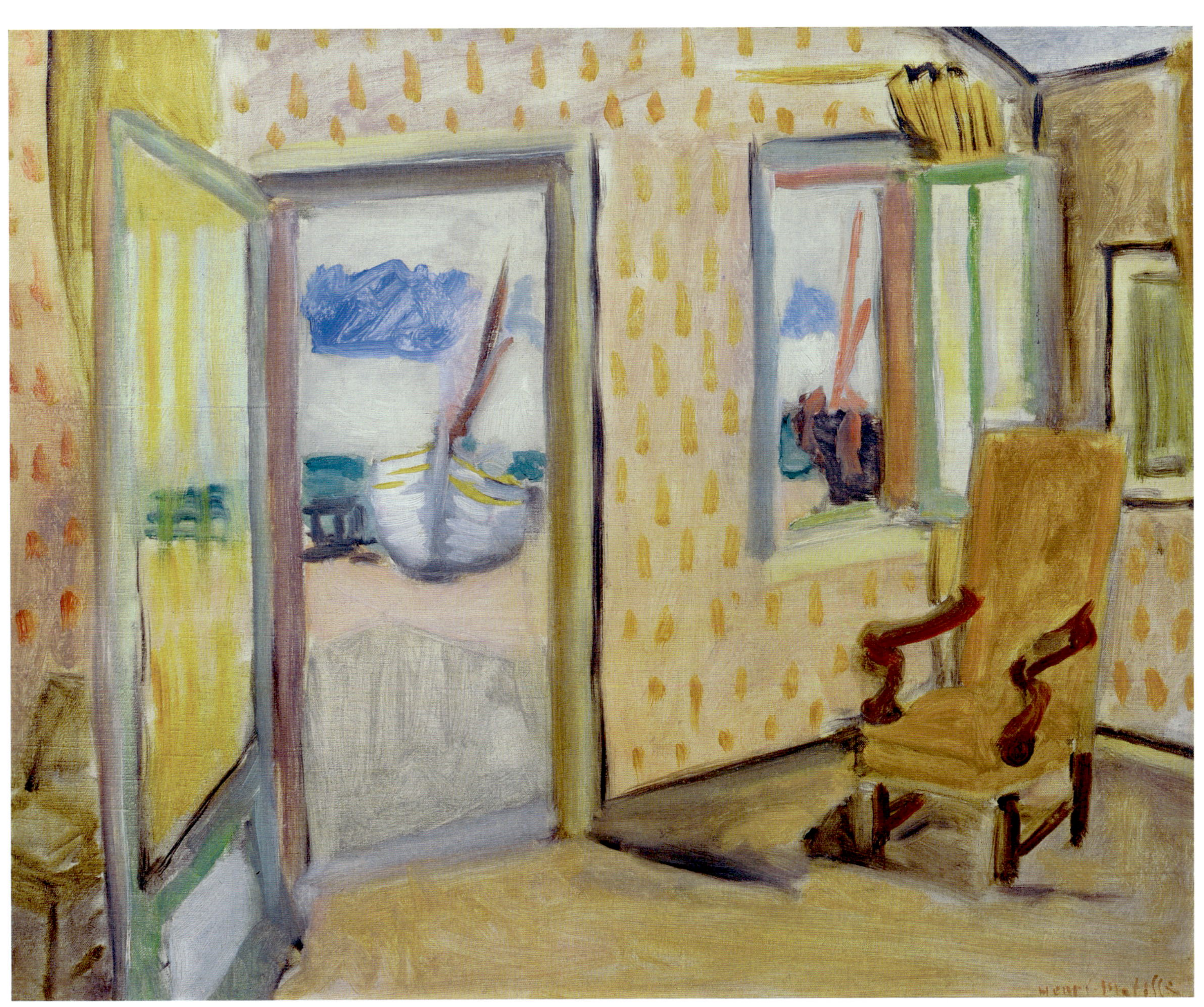

Grande tête, chevelure
Executed in 1947
Charcoal on paper
20¼ × 15¹⁵/₁₆ inches (51.4 × 40.5 cm)
Signed and dated lower right: *Henri Matisse avril 47*
28022-001

PROVENANCE
Estate of the artist
Pierre and Maria-Gaetana Matisse Foundation
Hammer Galleries, New York
Private collection, Los Angeles
Hammer Galleries, New York

EXHIBITED
Hammer Galleries, New York, *Works on Paper, Chagall, Matisse, Miró, Picasso,*
    April 21–May 17, 2004, illustrated pp. 20–21.

This work is accompanied by a photo-certificate of authenticity dated Paris 12/2/2004 from
Mme. Wanda de Guébriant stating the piece is numbered M182 in the archives of the artist.

"My models, human figures, are never just 'extras' in an interior. They are the principal
theme in my work. I depend entirely on my model, whom I observe at liberty, and then
I decide on the pose that best suits her nature. When I take a new model, I intuit the pose
that will best suit her from her un-selfconscious attitudes of repose, and then I become
the slave of that pose. I often keep those girls several years, until my interest is exhausted.
My plastic signs probably express their souls (a word I dislike), which interests me
subconsciously, or what else is there? Their forms are not always perfect, but they are always
expressive. The emotional interest aroused in me by them does not appear particularly
in the representation of their bodies, but often rather in the lines or the special values
distributed over the whole canvas or paper, which forms its complete orchestration, its
architecture. But not everyone perceives this. It is perhaps sublimated sensual pleasure,
which may not yet be perceived by everyone" (Henri Matisse, *Notes of a Painter on his
Drawing, 1939,* quoted in Jack Flam, ed., *Matisse on Art,* Berkeley, 1994, p. 81).

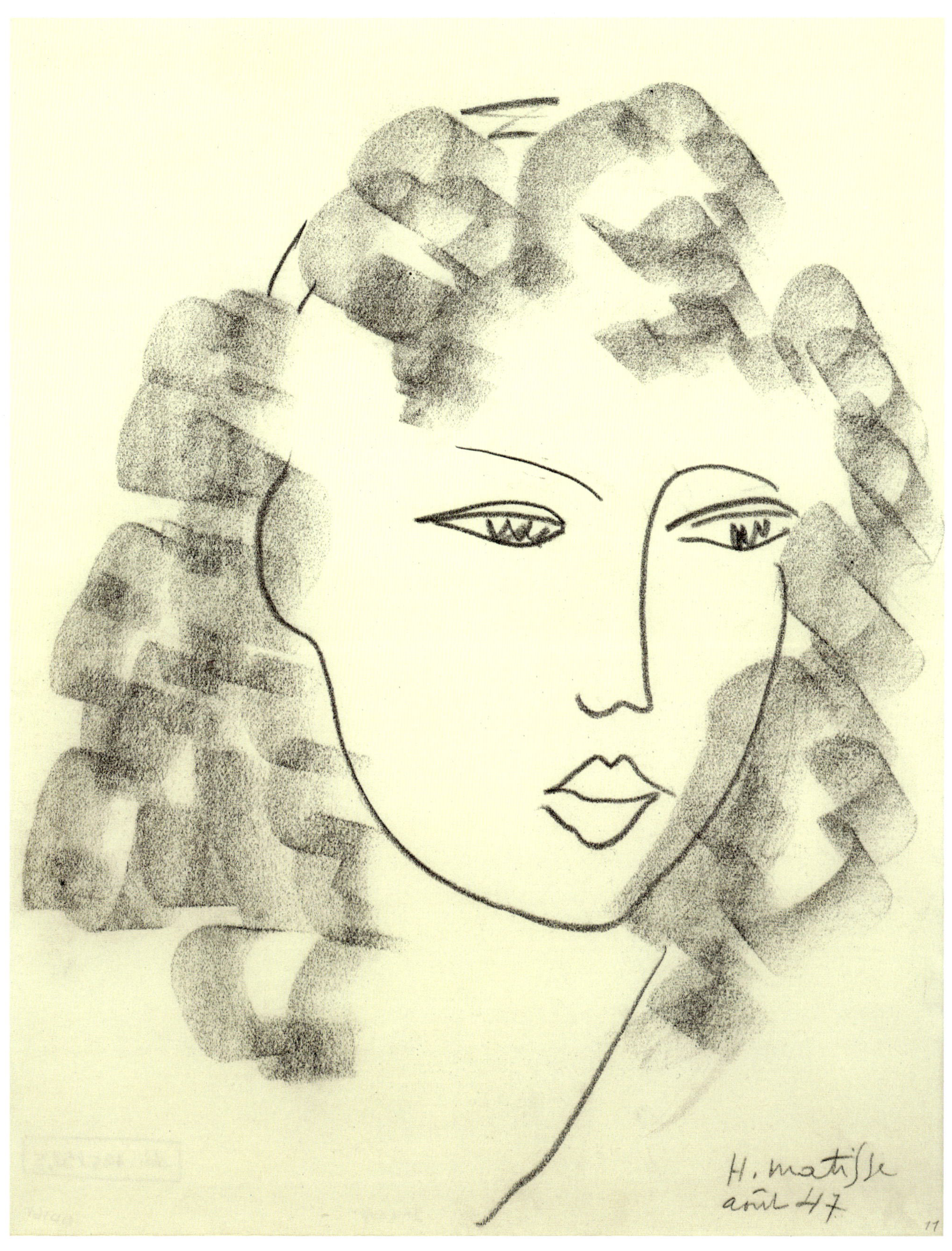

H. matisse
août 47

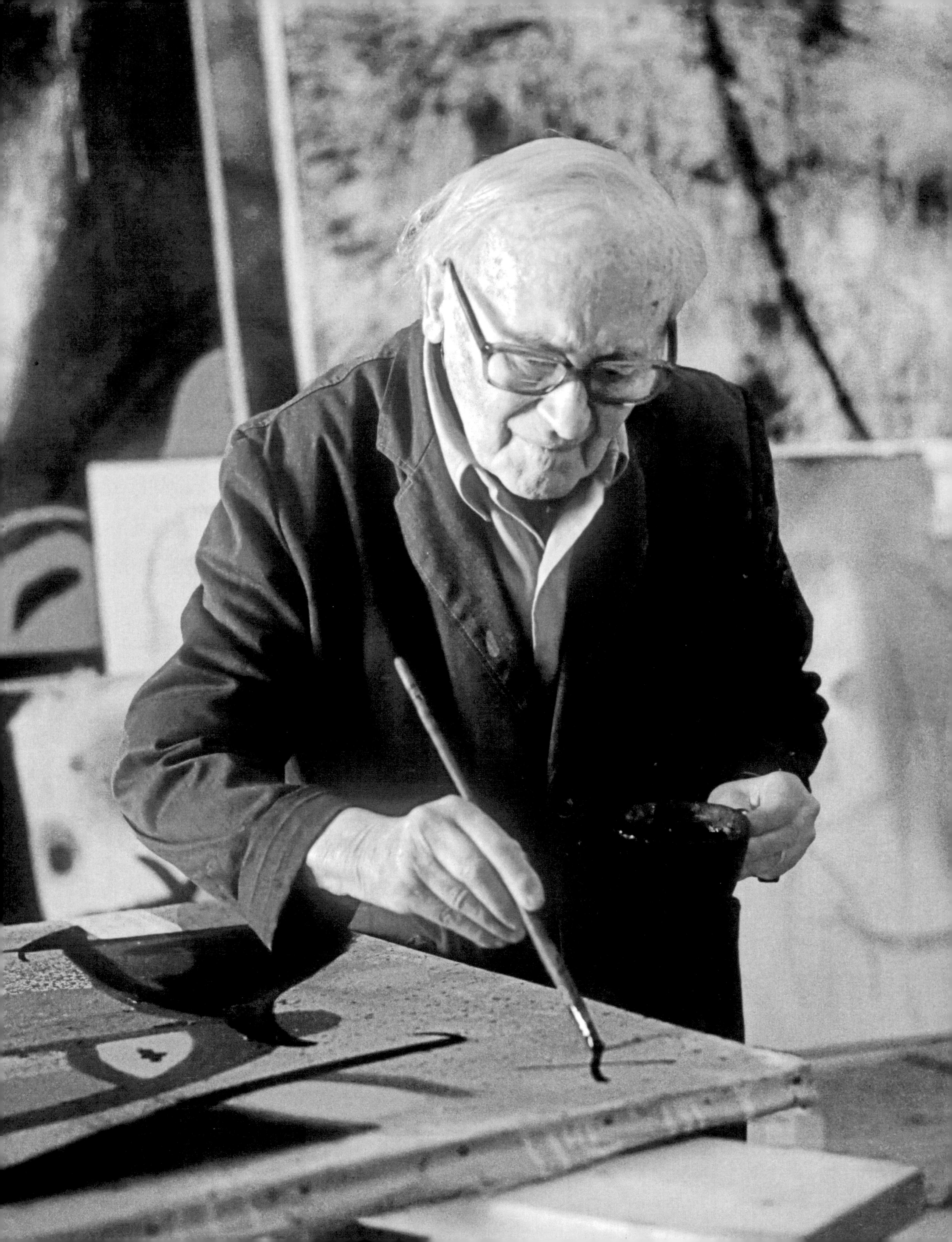

Miró was one of the most influential artists of the 20th century, but his work is in some way difficult to place in terms of 20th century " isms." Born in Barcelona, he was the son of a prosperous goldsmith and locksmith. From childhood he was attracted to the visual arts. He remembered later that the art classes he took after school were "for me like a religious ceremony. I washed my hands carefully before touching the paper and crayons. The artist's tools were sacred objects for me, and I worked as if I was participating in a rite." Nevertheless his family was unsympathetic to his wish to establish himself as an artist, and he was only able to liberate himself in slow stages.

His first glimpse of what was happening in Paris occurred when the French dealer Ambroise Vollard sent an important loan show of recent French paintings to Barcelona, and he was confronted by the work of Monet, Cézanne and Matisse. Shortly after that, he met the leading Dadaist Francis Picabia. In 1919 he went to Paris himself, where he met Picasso. Thereafter he started to divide his time between Paris and Montroig in Catalonia, where his family had a house.

In Paris, he encountered the Surrealists. He never became an official member of the Surrealist group, though he did participate in the first Surrealist Exhibition, held in November 1925 at the Galerie Pierre, where Miró had a solo show a few months earlier. His style, by this time, had begun to be influenced by the work of Paul Klee, whose work was just becoming known in France. The amalgamation of Surrealist influence with that of Klee led Miró to produce what are still some of his best-known works, a series of *Dutch Interiors* that are fantastic paraphrases of 17th-century Dutch genre-paintings.

By 1930 Miró was well enough known to have his first show in America. Thereafter American patronage played an important role in his work, though he never went to live there.

In Paris, Miró had played a minor political role as an opponent of Franco during the Spanish Civil War. For example, he designed a mural for the Spanish Pavilion at the Paris Exposition Universelle of 1937. This was the building that also housed Picasso's *Guernica*. The German invasion of France forced him to return to Spain with his family. Fearful of attracting attention from the now triumphant Franco regime, he took refuge with his wife's family in Majorca.

At this crucial point in his career, America came to his rescue. In 1941, he was given a large retrospective exhibition at the Museum of Modern Art in New York. After the war ended he continued to receive generous American patronage, painting a large mural for a hotel in Cincinnati, then another for the Graduate School at Harvard. In 1959, he had a second retrospective at the Museum of Modern Art. Meanwhile he had gradually discovered that living in Spain had distinct advantages for an artist who liked a quiet life but whose fame was growing rapidly. Since he was out of favor with the regime, he was ignored by the Spanish press. He based himself in Barcelona from 1942 to 1956, then settled in Palma, Majorca, where he lived the rest of his long and productive life.

The works shown here are all from the later phases of his career. He never stopped experimenting with new forms and new techniques. Sculpture, for example, became an increasing preoccupation. The powerful *Figure*, made when Miró was in his 80s, has an obvious affinity with Dubuffet's 'Art Brut.' The group of ceramic pieces illustrates Miró's constant playfulness and his wry sense of humor. A number of the Modern Masters of the École de Paris worked with ceramics— Picasso and Léger are other examples. What they seem to have liked was the opportunity to return to basic artisanal values—clay was the most basic possible medium for making art, known in every period of human development and in all cultures. The little ceramic *Oeuf* is art reduced to its most basic state, but Miró's special creative magic is still present.

Joan Miró in his studio, Palma, Majorca, Spain, March 3, 1979

Personnage au nez rouge
Executed in 1956
Unique painted and glazed assembled ceramic
17⅝ × 13⅜ × 5¾ inches (44 × 33 × 14.5 cm)
Signed on reverse: *Miró / ARTIGAS*
28025-001

PROVENANCE
Galerie Maeght, Paris
Pierre Matisse Gallery, New York
Mr. & Mrs. Morton Neumann, Chicago
Perls Gallery, New York
Knickerbocker Fine Arts Collection, New York
Hammer Galleries, New York

LITERATURE
José Pierre & José Corredor-Matheos, *Céramiques de Miró et Artigas*, Maeght, Paris, 1974,
    no. 222, illustrated p. 96 (titled *Plaque relief*).
Francesc Miralles, *Llorens Artigas*, Ediciones Polígrafa, Barcelona, 1992, no. 768, p. 307,
    illustrated.
Daniel Lelong & Successió Miró, Miró-Artigas, *Ceramics, Catalogue Raisonné, 1941–1981*,
    Le Coudray, 2007, no. 258, illustrated p. 216 (titled *Plaque with Relief*, material listed as
    earthenware).

In 1944, Miró began to work in Barcelona with his friend, the potter Josep Llorens Artigas.
The medium of clay had fascinated him for several years and after his recent and highly
successful series of *Constellations* on paper and canvas, he turned to this medium as a new
challenge.

    As José Pierre notes, this medium was also a bridge between painting and sculpture:
"Since his very first contact with the medium, it was clear that working in ceramic satisfied
two distinct impulses within him; one pictorial in nature, the other more specifically
sculptural. In both cases, however, working in ceramic introduced very particular qualities,
ones that distinguished Miró's ceramic paintings from his paintings *per se*, and his ceramic
sculptures from those made in bronze and cement. 'It was the luster of ceramic that
seduced me; it almost sparkles,' he said" (pp. 11–12).

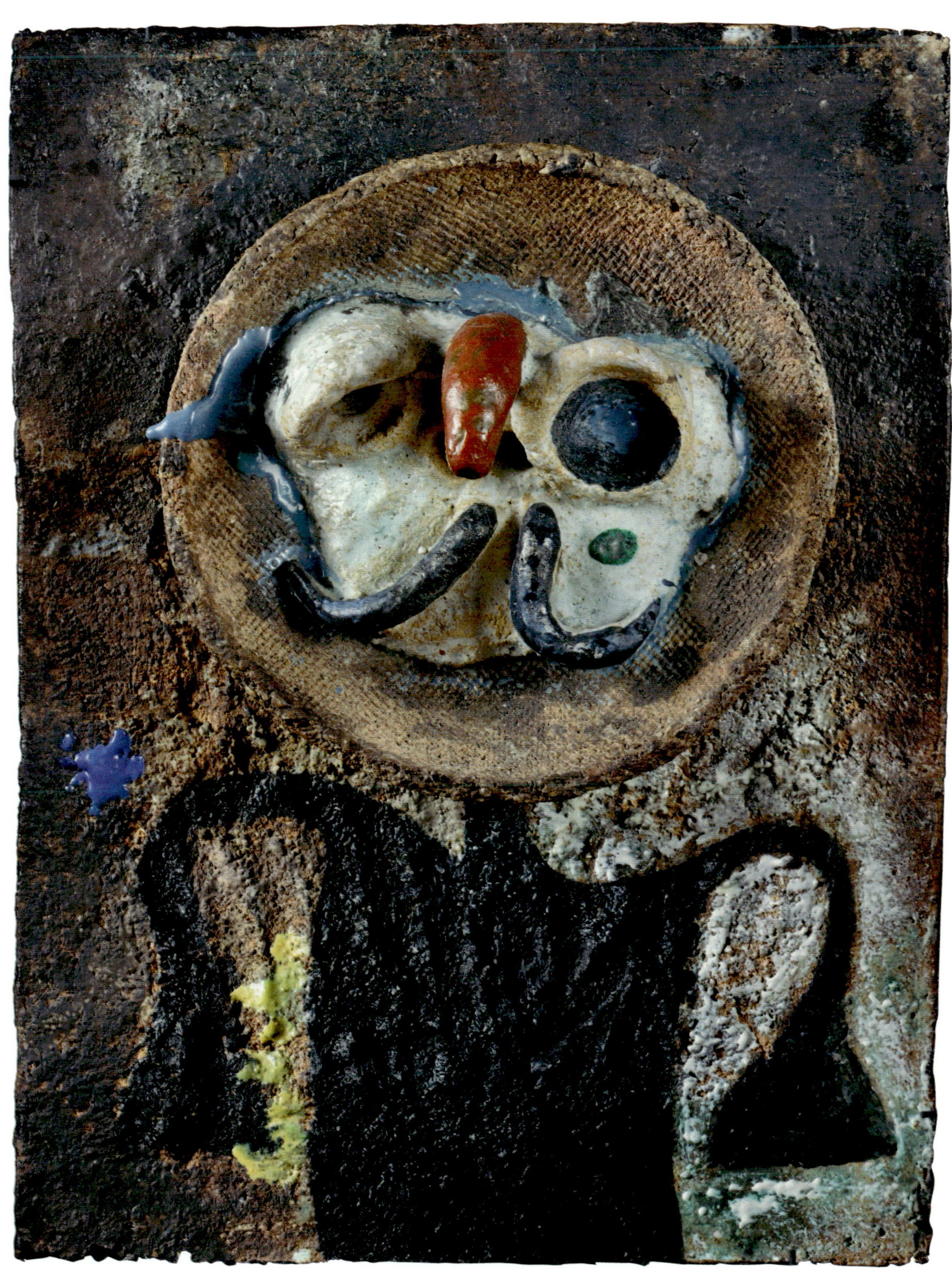

Figurine (Projet pour un monument)
Executed in 1956
Unique painted iron and partially glazed ceramic
17¾ × 4⅜ inches (45 × 11 cm)
Signed on the underside: *Miró / ARTIGAS*
28026-009

PROVENANCE
Pierre Matisse Gallery, New York
Perls Galleries, New York
Mr. and Mrs. H. Gates Lloyds, Haverford, Pennsylvania (acquired from the above in May 1982)
Acquired by the present owner in 1994

EXHIBITED
Tokyo, National Museum of Modern Art and Kyoto, National Museum of Modern Art,
    Joan Miró, 1966, cat. no. 142, illustrated p. 160.
Paris, Grand Palais: *Joan Miró*, 1974, cat. no. 297, p. 165, illustrated.

LITERATURE
José Pierre & José Corredor-Matheos, *Céramiques de Miró et Artigas*, Maeght, Paris, 1974,
    no. 53, illustrated p. 64.
Francesc Miralles, *Llorens Artigas*, Barcelona, 1992, no. 726, illustrated p. 295.
Daniel Lelong & Successió Miró, *Miró-Artigas, Ceramics, Catalogue Raisonné, 1941–1981*,
    Le Coudray, 2007, no. 68, illustrated p. 81 (material listed as stoneware and iron).

Jacques Dupin was a French poet, art critic, and close friend of Miró. In his biography of
the artist, Dupin describes the nature of Miró's fascination with the ceramic medium: "What
attracted Miró to ceramics was indeed its element of surprise and the unpredictability that
transforms the work in process. From beginning to end, it engages the work in a kind of
living metamorphosis, continually upsetting the creator's calculations, and compelling him
to adjust to its slightest reaction, to confront it over and over again from a new perspective.
Miró wrote: 'In spite of all the precautions one can take, however, the ultimate master of the
work is fire. Its actions are unpredictable, and its power can be deadly. This is what creates
the value of this means of expression'" (Jacques Dupin, *Miró*, Paris: Flammarion, 2004, p. 392).

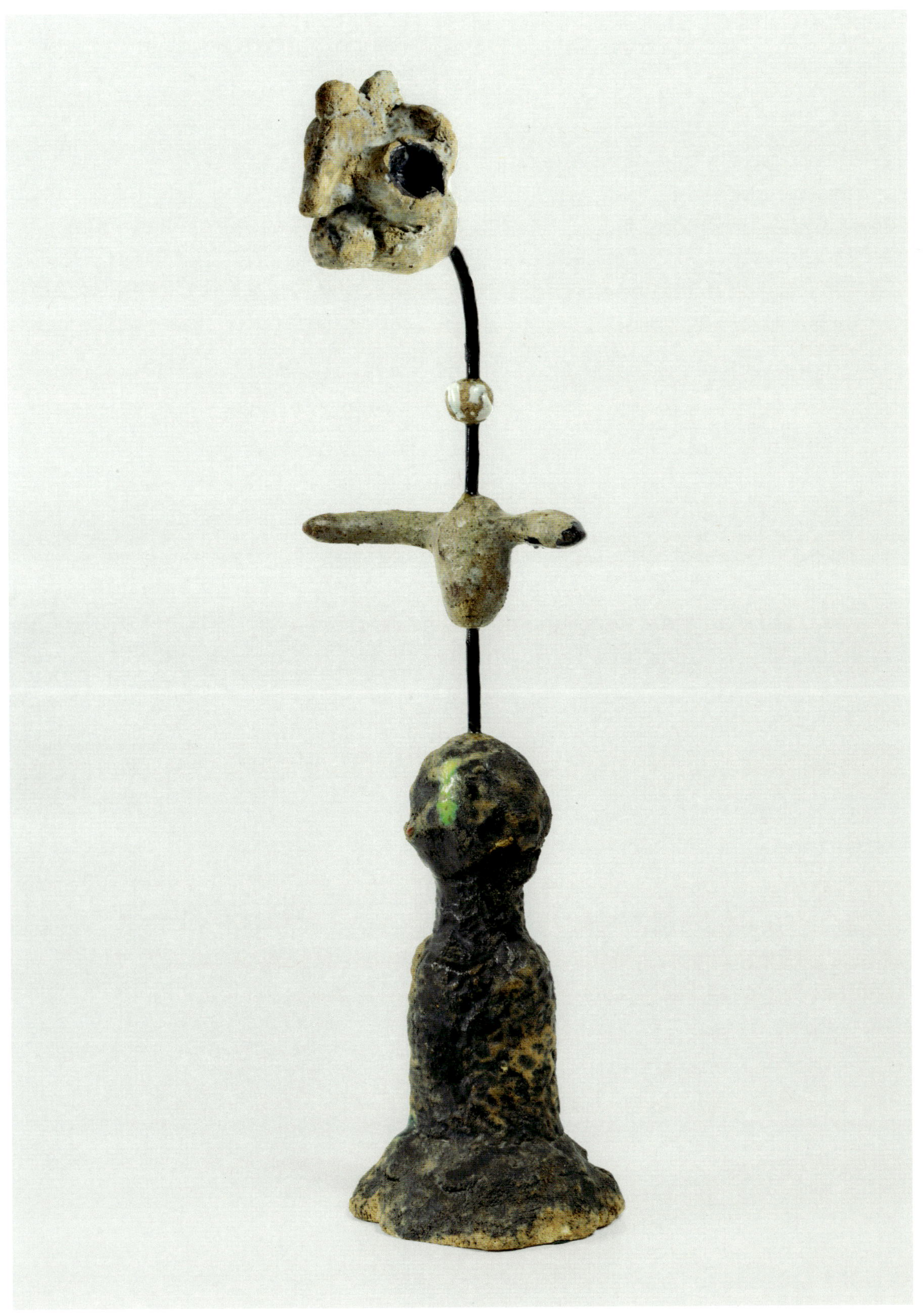

Oeuf
Executed circa 1956
Unique painted ceramic
Height: 2¼ inches (5.5 cm)
Signed on the bottom: *Miró / ARTIGAS*
28026-010

PROVENANCE

Galerie Maeght, Paris
The Mary Woodard Lasker Charitable Trust, New York (acquired from the above on
    September 16, 1968)
The Stanley J. Seeger Collection (1995–2001)
Acquired by the present owner in 2001

EXHIBITED

Tokyo, National Museum of Modern Art and Kyoto, National Museum of Modern Art,
    Joan Miró, 1966, cat. no. 160, p. 133, illustrated.

LITERATURE

Daniel Lelong & Successió Miró, *Miró-Artigas, Ceramics, Catalogue Raisonné, 1941–1981*,
    Le Coudray, 2007, no. 141, illustrated p. 136 (material listed as stoneware).

In working with ceramics, Miró intentionally strayed from the traditional aspect of the craft. His "humor and playfulness were manifested above all in his invented or 'found' forms. . . . Among other things he decorated a large number of pebbles and a beautiful series of eggs" (Jacques Dupin, *Miró*, Paris: Flammarion, 2004, p. 390).

Roland Penrose asserts that "it is perhaps when at work on ceramics that Miró enjoys most completely the full scope of his genius. There is no facet in the wide range of his talents that does not come into play. . . . Ceramics are for Miró an extension of both painting and sculpture, in which many of his discoveries in both arts can be combined. There is everything in this art to enchant him" (Roland Penrose, *Miró*, London: Thames and Hudson, 1985, p. 144).

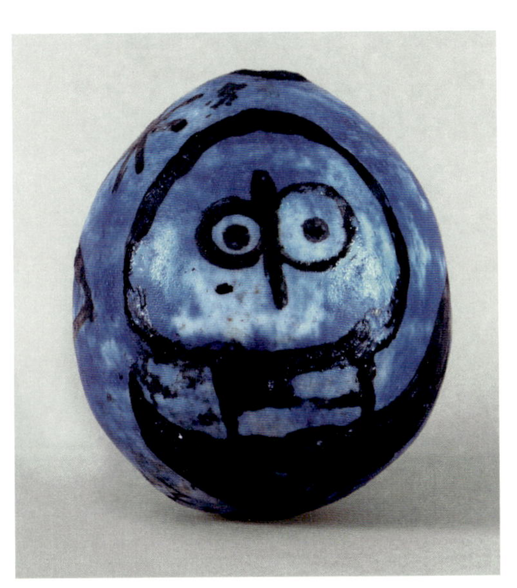 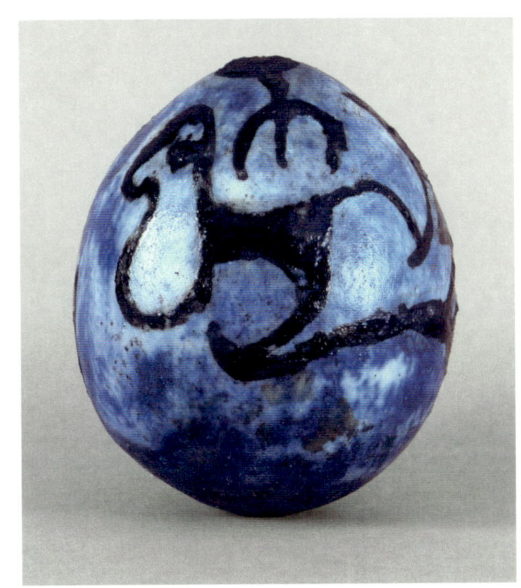

Femme et oiseau
Painted in 1966
Oil and casein tempera on canvas
$25^5/_8 \times 21^3/_8$ inches (65.2 × 54.3 cm)
Signed lower right: *Miró*
Signed, dated and tilted enverso: *Miró, 18/XI/66 Femme et Oiseau*
28031-010

PROVENANCE
Pierre Matisse Gallery, New York
Galerie Maeght, Paris
Acquired by the present owner in 1992

LITERATURE
Jacques Dupin & Ariane Lelong-Mainaud, *Joan Miró. Catalogue raisonné. Paintings. Vol IV:*
   1959–1968, Paris, 2002, no.1244, p.192, illustrated in color.

This work is accompanied by a photo-certificate signed by Jacques Dupin and dated Paris,
6 October 1992.

Femme et oiseau is one of several paintings on the theme of women and birds that Miró made
in the mid-1960s at a time when he was exploring the joint influences of recent American
abstract painting and of Japanese calligraphy on his own uniquely poetic, instinctive and
gestural style of painting. Jacques Dupin suggests that this motif "offers one of the keys to
Miró's cosmic imagination. It exposes conflict, and translates the unstable balance of the
heavenly and earthly into a struggle between woman and bird. . . . The analogy between the
two creatures and the intricacies of their lines are such that it is difficult to tell where the
woman ends and the bird begins or if they do not in fact form together a single marvelous
hybrid" (quoted in *Miró*, Solomon R. Guggenheim Museum, New York, 1987, p.51).
    The artist himself addressed the origin of this theme in relation to another painting:
"Where does that theme come from? Good Lord! Perhaps the bird comes from the fact that
I like space a lot and the bird makes one think of space. . . . It's always the same kind of
theme, my kind of theme" (quoted in Yvon Taillander, "Miró: Now I Work on the Floor" in
Margit Rowell (ed.), *Joan Miró Selected Writings and Interviews*, Cambridge, Massachusetts:
Da Capo Press, 1992, p. 283).

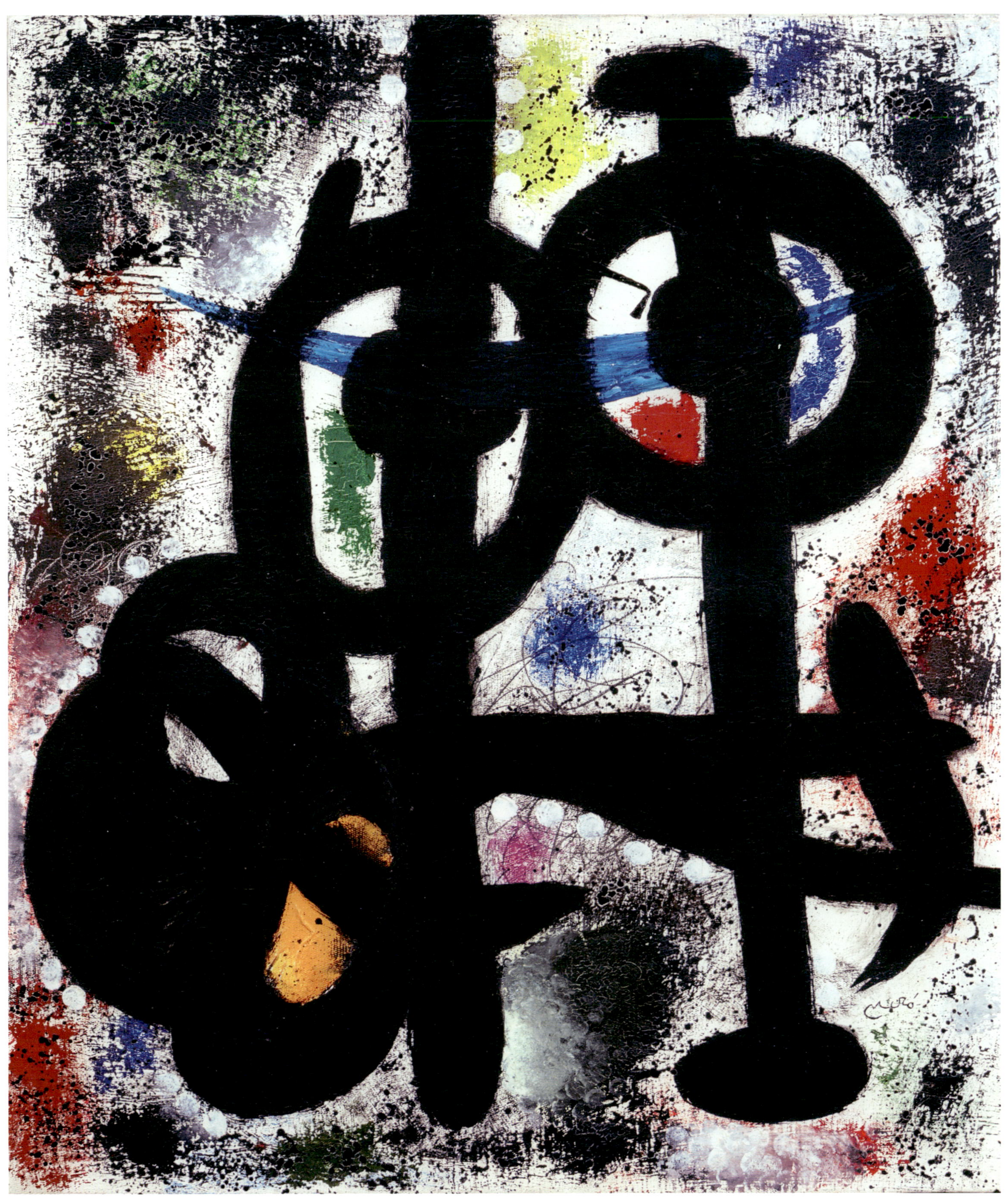

Figure
Executed in 1981
Bronze (lost wax casting), Fondacio Parellada
15 × 15³⁄₄ × 5¹⁄₂ inches (38 × 40 × 14 cm)
Signed lower right: *Miró 1/6*
28027-001

PROVENANCE
Pierre Matisse Gallery, New York
The Pierre and Maria Gaetana Matisse Foundation
Acquired by the present owner circa 2005

EXHIBITED
Palma, Pelaires Cultural Contemporani, 1993, p. 42, illustrated p. 43.

LITERATURE
Emilio Fernandez Miró and Pilar Ortega Chapel, *Miró Sculptures, Catalogue Raisonné*,
    Ediciones Polígrafa, Barcelona, 2006, number 387, illustrated p. 358.

Miró began making free-standing sculptures and collaborating with Josep Artigas,
a noted ceramist and friend, while living in Palma, Montroig and Barcelona during
World War II. In his *Working Notes, 1941–1942,* Miró wrote, "It is in sculpture that I
will create a truly phantasmagoric world of living monsters; what I do in painting
is more conventional" (in Margit Rowell, (ed.), *Joan Miró: Selected Writings and
Interviews,* Boston, 1986, p. 175).

As Jacques Dupin notes: "When the bronze has melted, cooled and been delivered
from its plaster womb, what are these figures that stand before us? Difficult to identify,
despite their affirmation and because of their intensity. Neither men nor beasts, nor
monsters nor intermediate creatures, but with something of all of these. Their aggressive
presence is a blend of the grotesque and the incongruous, of predatory fascination and
the artlessness of the primitive game. The unfailing laughter of these creatures freezes
before bursting out; it is in us, beyond us, that it tears the walls and the sky. We feel its
commotion as it passes, its charge of dynamite in suspense and a sinking of the ground
under its passage, a trembling in the air, a tumult of freshness" (in *Miró as Sculptor,*
Barcelona, 1976, pp. 25–26).

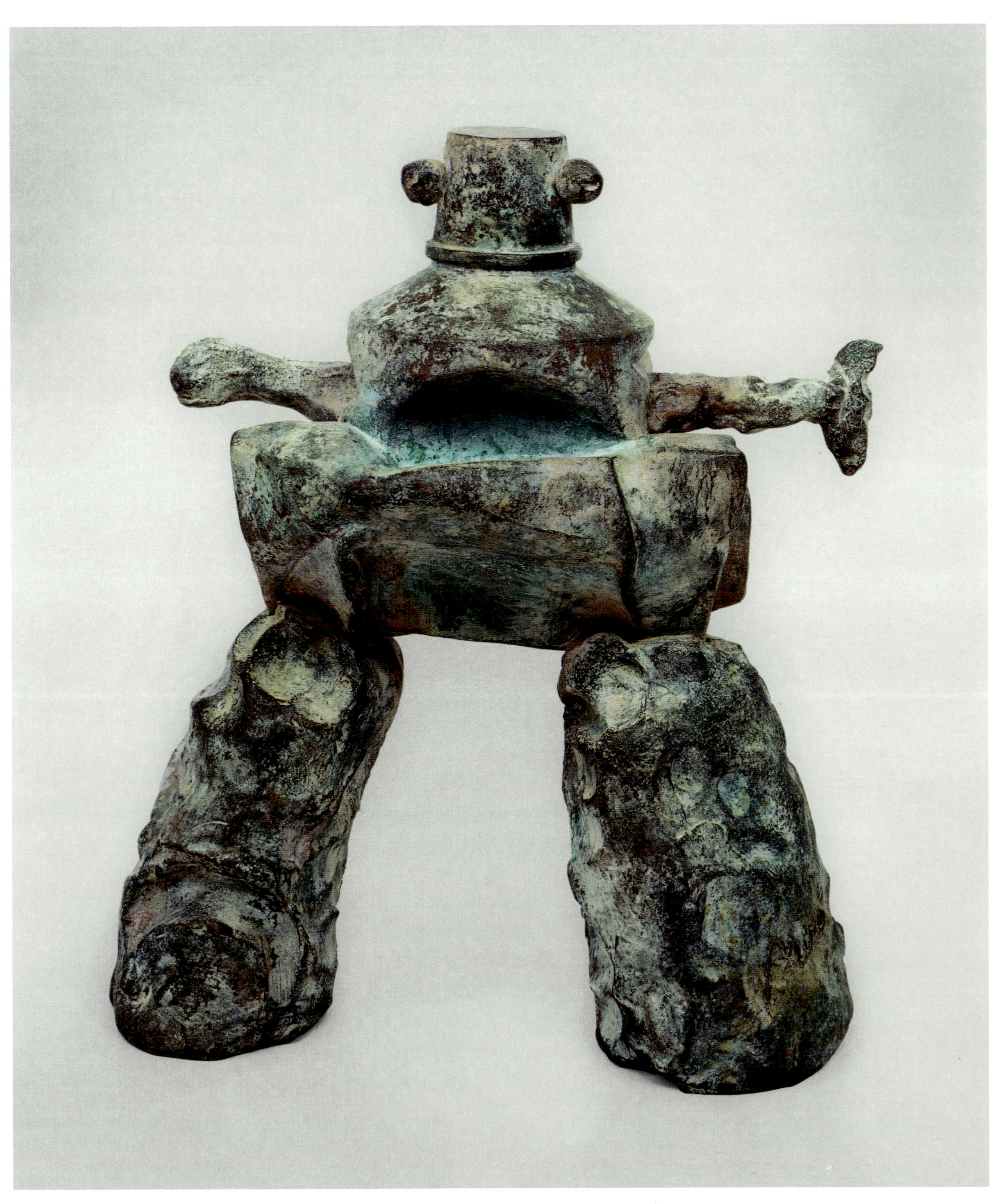

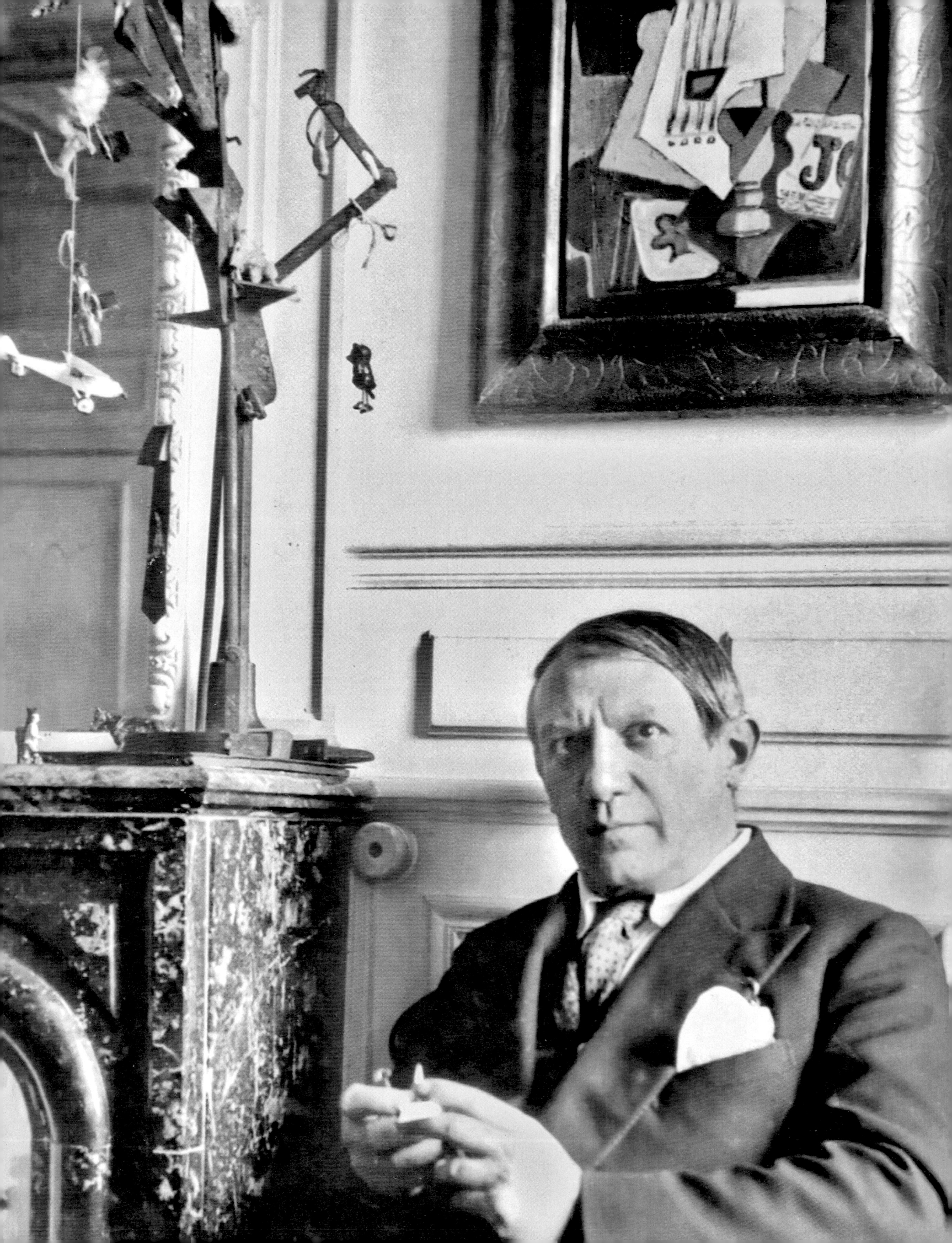

PABLO PICASSO (Spanish, 1881–1973)

Picasso is the most prodigious, the most inventive, the most varied of all the masters of 20th-century art. Most people would agree in calling him the most important, comparable in his cultural context to Michelangelo in the 16th century. Born in Malaga in 1881, he spent the first period of his artistic career in Barcelona, culturally the liveliest city in Spain. In 1900 he paid his first visit to Paris, and in the opening years of the 20th century went back and forth between Paris, Madrid and Barcelona. His first fully mature works—the paintings of the so-called Blue and Rose Periods owed a good deal to the Europe–wide Symbolist Movement. In 1906 Picasso, influenced by his discovery of African tribal art, experienced an extraordinary creative explosion, which led, in 1906–7, to the creation of what is still, perhaps, his best-known painting, *Les Demoiselles d'Avignon*. This led, in turn, to the birth of Cubism, an artistic movement in which Picasso, together with his friend Georges Braque, were the leading figures.

Picasso continued to develop his new Cubist style throughout the grim years of World War I, often working in isolation. However, he also formed a link with the exiled Ballets Russes company, led by the Russian impresario Serge Diaghilev. This opened his mind to a range of new stylistic possibilities, but also returned his thoughts to the great painters of the past.

During the interwar years Picasso's reputation increased rapidly as a result of his link to the Surrealist movement and his support for the Republican cause in the Spanish Civil War. The Republican Government made him Honorary Director of the Prado Museum, and Picasso reciprocated by painting the huge canvas *Guernica*, which was shown in the Spanish Pavilion at the Paris Exposition Universelle and was afterwards sent on tour. The composition is a bitter condemnation of the bombing of the Basque capital by Franco's German allies.

Picasso spent the bleak years of World War II living in virtual seclusion in Paris, untroubled by the German occupiers. After the war, he went to live in the south of France, in part because of its seductive climate, in part because moving there enabled him to escape from his now overwhelming celebrity. The subject matter of his work became increasingly self-reflexive—his major subjects were what it was to be an artist, and the enclosed life of the studio.

The works exhibited here begin with *Guitare sur un guéridon devant une fenêtre ouverte*, a fine Synthetic Cubist still life with a typical subject. Picasso often seems to have seen guitars as metaphors for the female body. This exquisite miniature painting belonged to the American sculptor Mary Callery and has a silver case designed for it by Julio González, the major Spanish sculptor who taught Picasso the craft of metal-smithing. The cover plate has a delightful image of a full-length figure, also Cubist in style, which is the work of Picasso himself. The work is effectively two Picassos in one. There follow two neoclassical works *Trois femmes à la fointaine* (1921), which represents this stylistic moment in its purest form, and the later *Le joueur de clarinette*, which is more romantic and turbulent. The female nude in this was inspired by Picasso's beautiful young mistress, Marie-Thérèse Walter. It was done at a time when their love-affair was still a secret from Picasso's notoriously jealous Russian wife.

Two works from the time after World War II give evidence of Picasso's strong sense of humor. In *Tête d'homme et nu assis* the male figure, though bearded, is clearly intended to be a self-portrait. Picasso often wore the sailor's striped jersey seen here. He confronts what was still a favorite subject for his art—the female nude—but this time she is generic rather than specific. *Le peintre* is not a self-portrait, but is, instead, a kind of riff on the physiognomy of Velazquez, the renowned painter whom Picasso revered yet, typically, regarded as a rival. This slightly disheveled *hidalgo* offers us Picasso's sardonic view of the world inhabited by the great Spanish painters who were his predecessors. It acknowledges them, but at the same time issues a challenge.

Pablo Picasso in Paris, circa 1930

PABLO PICASSO

Guitare sur un guéridon devant une fenêtre ouverte
Painted in 1919
Tempera on panel set in a silver frame
6⅝ × 4¾ inches (16.8 × 12 cm)
Signed and dedicated enverso: *Pour Mme Callery 1921*
28031-013

PROVENANCE
Mary Callery, New York (the sculptress)
Maria Martins, New York and South America (the sculptress, a gift from the above)
Private collection (by descent from above)
Acquired by the present owner in 1989

LITERATURE
Christian Zervos, *Pablo Picasso, Oeuvres de 1917 à 1919*, Paris, 1949, vol. 3, no. 422, illustrated
    p. 141 with incorrect measurements.
The Picasso Project, *Picasso's Paintings, Watercolors, Drawings and Sculptures: From Cubism to
    Neoclassicism, 1917–1919*, San Francisco, 1995, no. 19-320, illustrated p. 269.

Although this piece dates from a slightly later period, it is closely linked with Picasso's
Guitar series created between 1912 and 1914, recently the subject of an exhibition at the
Museum of Modern Art, New York (February 13–June 6, 2011).

The guitar is a recurring motif throughout Picasso's work of the 1910s and 1920s. "For
Picasso, the guitar was the king of Cubist musical instruments, as well as being a ubiquitous
presence in both his pre- and post-Cubist works. . . . Its isolation by Picasso as a virtual
emblem was conspicuous in 1912, when the guitar became the fundamental motif for his
adventurous new assembled sculptures." (Jonathan Brown, (ed.), *Picasso and the Spanish
Tradition*, New Haven, 1996, pp. 78–79).

This work is presented in a silver frame with a cover etched with a female figure by
Picasso. The previous owner recalls Mary Callery as saying that the frame was designed by
Picasso's friend Julio González, the Spanish sculptor. González is considered one of the
pioneers of contemporary sculpture in metal. After studying in Barcelona, González moved
to Paris in 1900 where he became a member of Picasso's circle. Through his collaborations
with Picasso, González taught him the traditional Spanish techniques of metal-work.

Mary Callery (born in New York, 1903) first met Picasso and Zervos in Paris while she
was a pupil in the studio of the sculptor Jacques Loutchansky. In speaking of her experience
with Picasso, Callery wrote, "The more one saw, the greater he became. I find myself even
now repeating the things I became aware of through him" (Mary Callery, "The Last Time I
Saw Picasso," 1942).

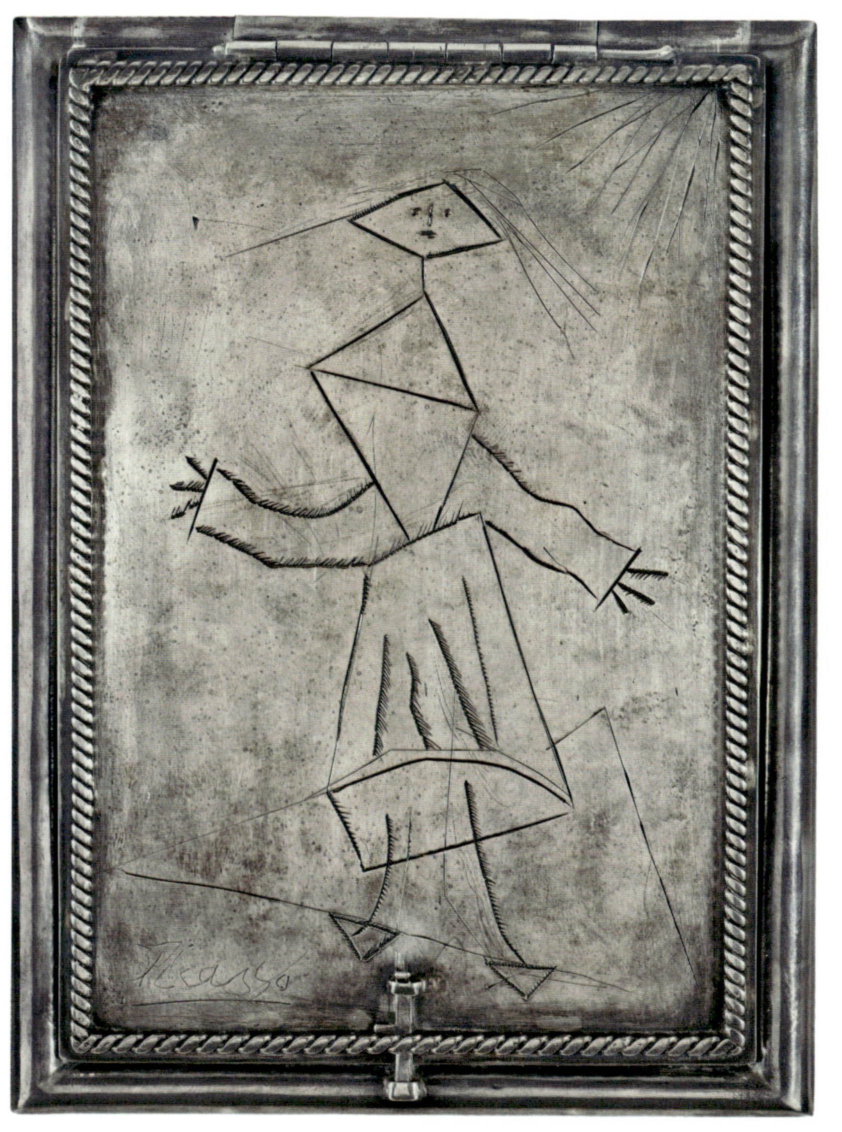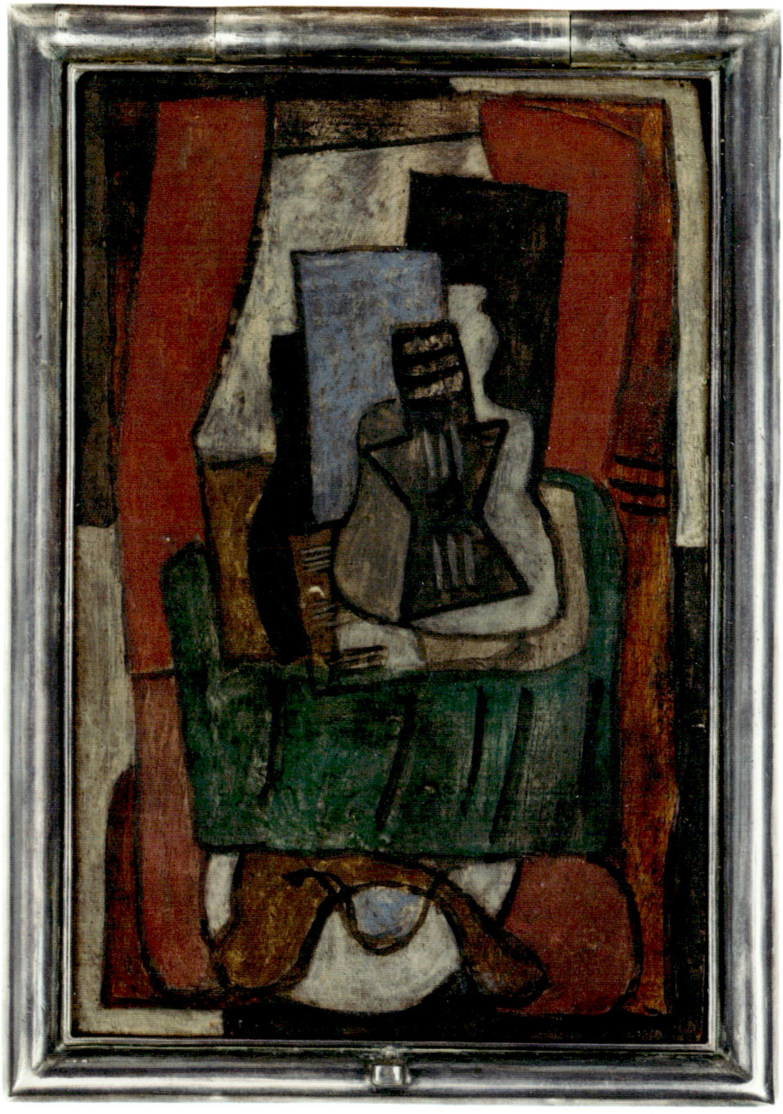

PABLO PICASSO

Trois femmes à la fontaine
Painted in 1921
Oil on canvas
8¾ × 13½ inches (22.3 × 34.3 cm)
28031-011

PROVENANCE
Estate of the artist
Claude Picasso, Paris
Galerie Claude Bernard, Paris
Acquavella Galleries, New York
Private collection
Acquired by the present owner in 1989

EXHIBITED
Paris, Galerie Claude Bernard, *Picasso, Peintures 1901–1971*, 1980, no.6, illustrated.
Humlebæk, Denmark, Louisiana Museum of Modern Art, *Picasso and the Mediterranean*,
    20 September 1996–19 January 1997, p.40, no.6, illustrated.
Rotterdam, Kunsthal, *Picasso—Artist of the Century*, 13 March–4 April, 1999, p.103, no.65,
    illustrated in color.
New York, C & M Arts, *Picasso: The Classical Period*, 1 October–6 December 2003, no.8,
    illustrated in color.

Trois femmes à la fontaine, painted in Fontainebleau in the summer of 1921, belongs to a
series of canvases of three women at a fountain, culminating in Picasso's *Three Women at
the Spring*, now at the Museum of Modern Art, New York (Zervos, vol. 4, no. 322). In his
discussion of the piece, MoMA curator Kirk Varnedoe explained, "When you look at
Picasso's *Three Women at the Spring* this represents the embodiment of what one calls
the return to order—the idea that after World War I, French society wanted to reestablish
its roots with the grand tradition and a kind of solid, reassuring, sculptural vision of the
human figure rooted in classicism. It was an art of reassurance, of regrounding after
the experimentation of the teens. And yet when you look at this picture, it's not really a
conservative picture—the tubular nature of the arms, the large abstract rhythms of the
figures are very much a legacy of Picasso's more radical work. . . . Picasso is happy working
in two extremes virtually simultaneously, painting a picture of strong Cubist abstraction on
the one hand and seemingly full bodied sculptural realism on the other," (Audio Program
excerpt, *Matisse Picasso*, February 13–May 19, 2003, The Museum of Modern Art, New York).

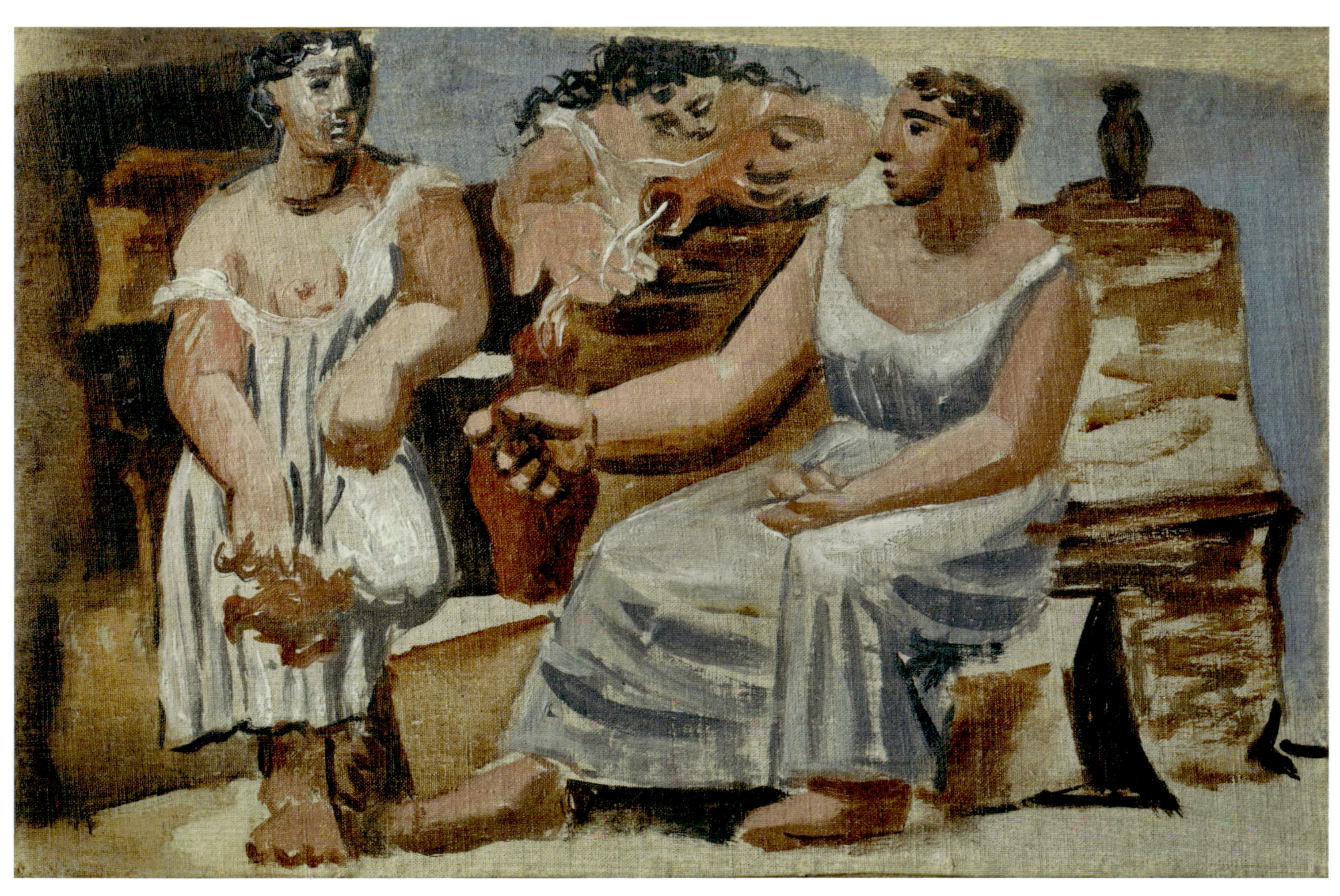

Le joueur de clarinette
Executed in 1932
Ink and wash on paper
10⅛ × 13 inches (25.8 × 33 cm)
Signed and dated lower left: *Picasso, Paris, 13 octobre–17 novembre XXXII*
28031-015

PROVENANCE
André Level collection
Private collection (by descent from above)
Acquired by the present owner in 2010

This work is accompanied by a certificate of authenticity signed by Maya Widmaier Picasso and dated Paris, 28th July 2010. It is also accompanied by a certificate of authenticity signed by Claude Ruiz Picasso and dated 10th May 2010.

Picasso's mistress, Marie-Thérèse Walter, is the subject of Picasso's well-known series of sleeping women, which he began in early 1932. Picasso's association with Marie-Thérèse began in 1927 (although some commentators claim they met earlier) when she was still a teenager living with her mother. Many years later she told *Life* magazine, "I was seventeen years old. I was an innocent young girl. I knew nothing—neither of life or of Picasso. Nothing. I had gone to do some shopping at the Galeries Lafayette, and Picasso saw me leaving the Metro. He simply took me by the arm and said: 'I am Picasso! You and I are going to do great things together'" (quoted in Pierre Daix, *Picasso: Life and Art*, New York, 1987, p. 202).

Robert Rosenblum has written: "In surveying the emotional and pictorial graph of Marie-Thérèse's covert and overt presence in Picasso's life and art, there is no doubt that 1932 marks the peak of fever-pitch intensity and achievement, a year of rapturous masterpieces that reach a new and unfamiliar summit in both his painting and sculpture" (in *Picasso and Portraiture*, (exhibition catalogue), The Museum of Modern Art, New York, 1996, p. 361).

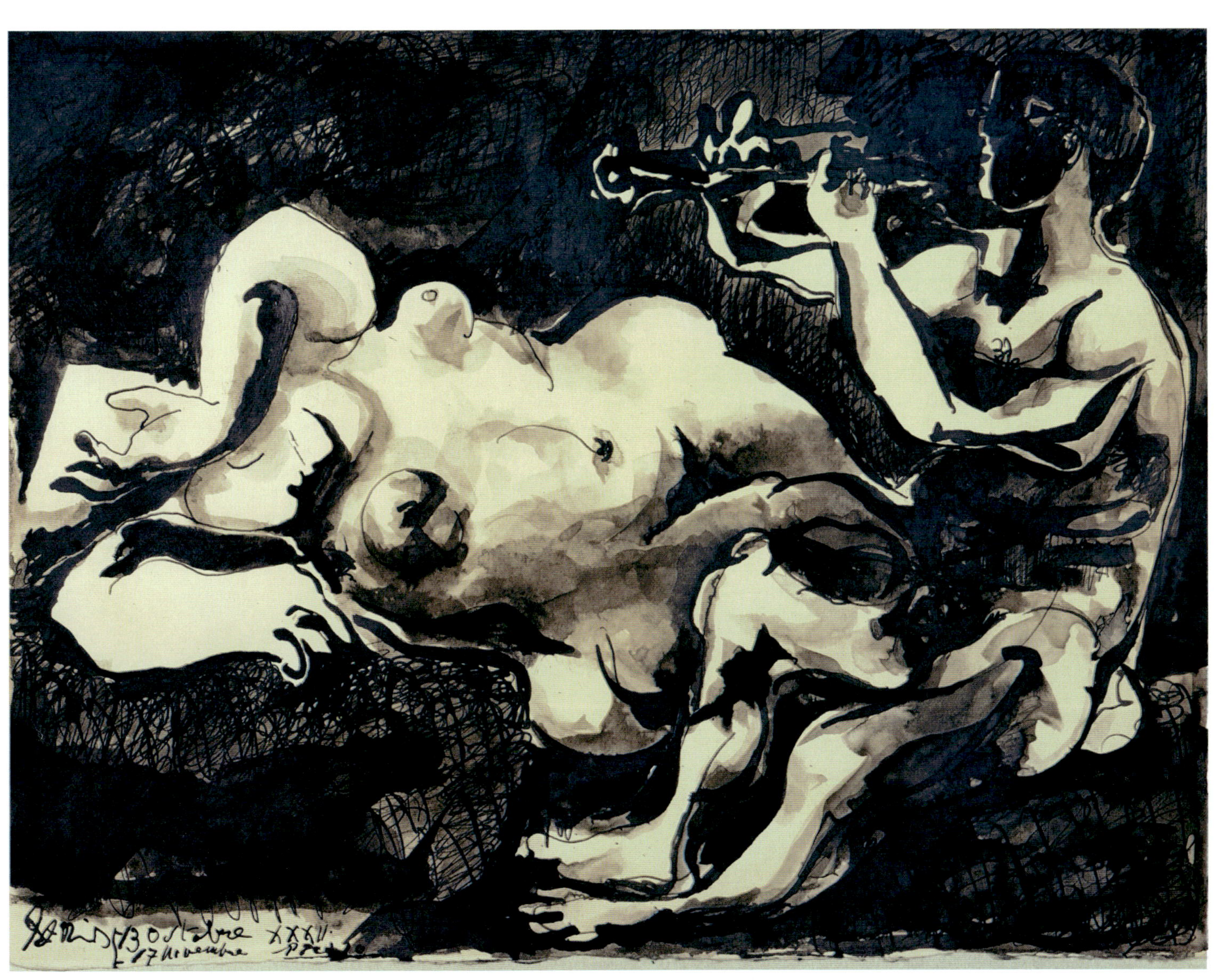

PABLO PICASSO

Tête de femme au chapeau
Executed in 1962
Wax crayon on paper
13¾ × 10⅝ inches (34.9 × 27 cm)
Signed, dated, and numbered upper left: *13.1.62 I Picasso*
28015-001

PROVENANCE
Galerie Rosengart, Lucerne (acquired directly from the artist)
Private collection, Germany (acquired from the above)
Private collection, Germany (by descent from the above)
Private collection, Great Britain
Hammer Galleries, New York
Private collection, New York

EXHIBITITED
Lucerne, Galerie Rosengart, *Picasso: An Idea Becomes Sculpture, variations on a theme*,
    July–September 1970, illustrated.*
Balingen, *Pablo Picasso: Portrait—Figurine—Skulptur*, June–August 1989, illustrated p. 123.
Balingen, *Pablo Picasso: Metamorphosen des Menschen*, June–September 2000, no. 140,
    illustrated.

LITERATURE
Christian Zervos, *Pablo Picasso, Ouvres de 1961 a 1962*, vol. XX, Paris, 1968, no. 193,
    illustrated p. 93, not signed.*
Graphis, 1970–71, no. 149, illustrated p. 11.
The Picasso Project, *Picasso's Paintings, Watercolors, Drawings and Sculpture: The Sixties I,
    1960–1963*, San Francisco, 2002, no. 62-014, illustrated p. 216, not signed.*

*Photo certificate signed in Lucerne, Switzerland by Dr. Angela Rosengart on May 21, 2011
stating, "I, Angela Rosengart, confirm that Pablo Picasso has signed the wax crayon drawing
'Tête de femme au chapeau' (reproduced at the reverse of this document) in the presence of
my father Siegfried Rosengart and me on October 18, 1970 after the exhibition 'Picasso, An
Idea Becomes Sculpture' shown in our gallery during the summer of 1970 to which Picasso
had loaned all the drawings."

Tête de femme au chapeau is a depiction of Jacqueline Roque (February 24, 1927–October 15,
1986), Picasso's second wife and his frequent model. Picasso and Jacqueline were married
in 1961 and remained together until Picasso's death in 1973. Jacqueline's image first
appeared in Picasso's work in May 1954 and became a repeated subject in his later works.

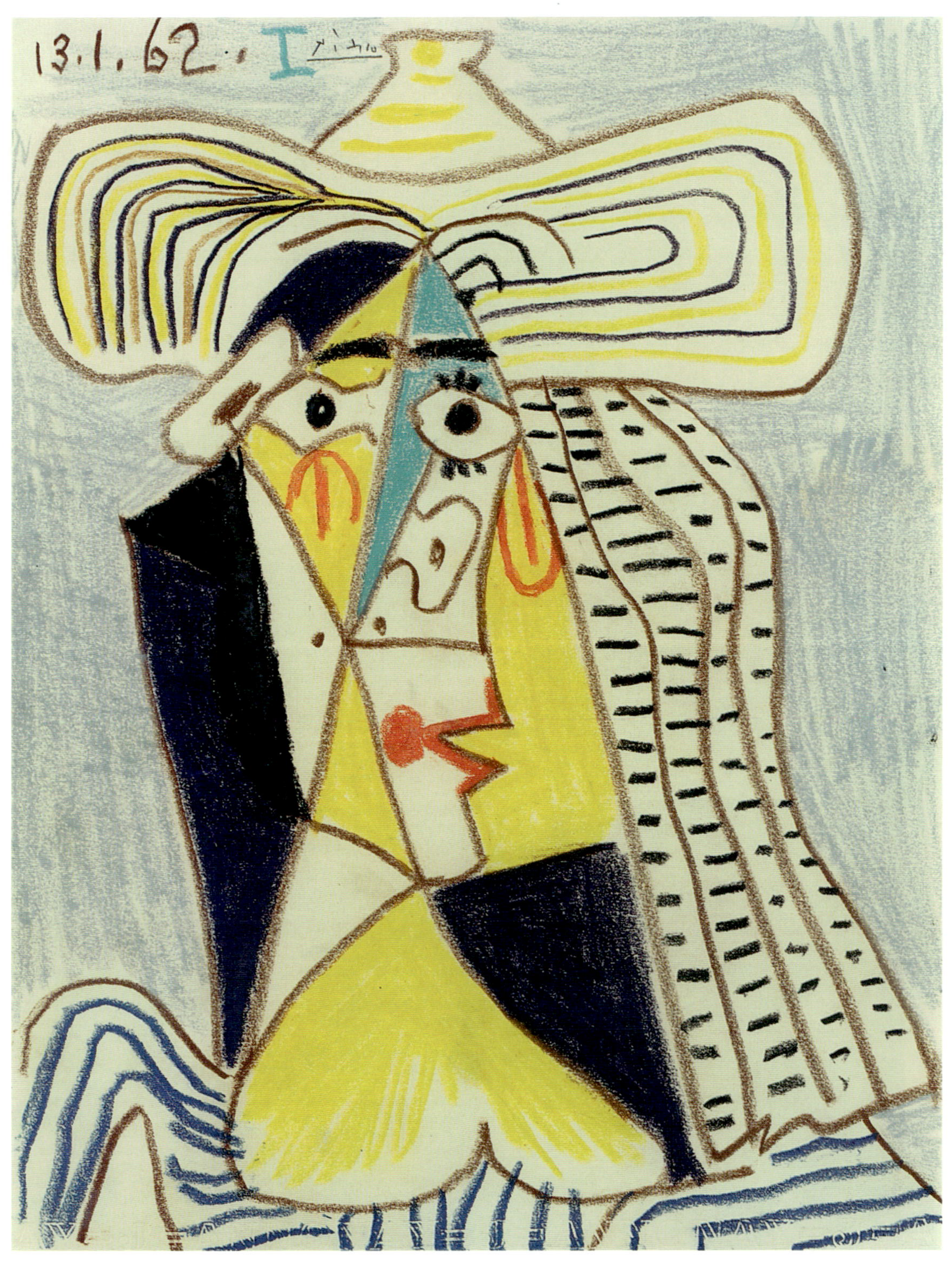

13.1.62. I

Tête d'homme et nu assis
Painted on November 24, 1964
Oil on canvas
25½ × 32 inches (65 × 81.2 cm)
Signed lower left: *Picasso*
Dated and numbered on the reverse: *24.11.64 III*
28031-012

PROVENANCE
Galerie Louise Leiris, Paris
Private collection
Acquired by the present owner in 1999

LITERATURE
Christian Zervos, *Pablo Picasso, Oeuvres de 1964*, Paris 1971, vol. 24, no.282, illustrated p.111.
The Picasso Project, *Picasso's Paintings, Watercolours, Drawings and Sculpture: The Sixties II,
    1964–1967*, San Francisco, 2002, no.64-282, p.90, illustrated.

The number of works created during Picasso's late period is so great that approximately
one third of the volumes of the Zervos *catalogue raisonné* are devoted to his final twenty
years. A recurrent theme during this period was that of the artist and model in the studio.

Helene Parmelin recalled, "Picasso went wild. He painted the artist and his model.
And from that moment on he painted like a mad thing, in a frenzy, as perhaps never
before. From February to May 1963, in January, October, November and December 1964,
and again in March 1965, paintings poured out one after another. In 1963 and 1964, he
painted almost nothing else: the painter, armed with his attributes, palette and brushes,
the canvas on an easel, mostly seen from the side, like a screen, and the nude model, seated
or reclining, in a space which presents all the characteristics of an artist's studio: the big
window, the sculpture on a stool, the folding screen, the lamp, the divan, etc. All these stage
props have nothing to do with Picasso's real situation; he always painted without a palette
and without an easel, directly onto a canvas laid flat" (quoted in M-L. Bernadac, "Picasso
1953–1972: Painting as Model," *Late Picasso*, London, 1988, p. 74).

Within this theme, Picasso painted numerous variations. Sometimes the model and
easel were depicted, in other works the artist is alone with his canvas, and still others—such
as this work—show only the artist and model. "Picasso now chose to work with isolated
figures, archetypes, and concentrated on the essential: the nude, the couple, man in disguise
or stripped bare: it was his way of dealing with the subject of women, love, and the human
comedy" (ibid., p. 78).

In several works from this series Picasso surrounds the couple with a frame painted
onto the canvas itself, calling attention to the painting's status as a work of art.

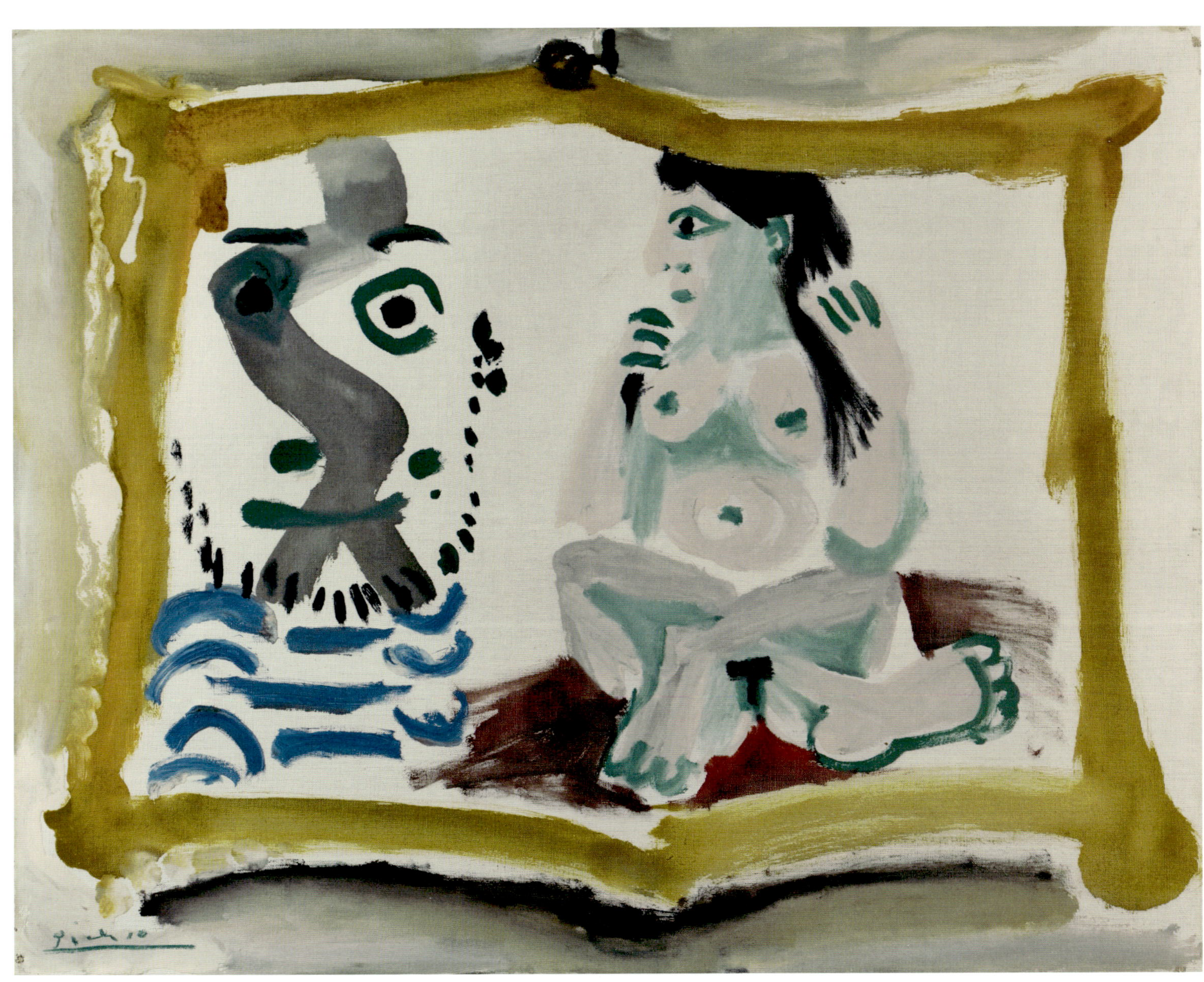

Le peintre
Painted on 25 March 1967
Oil on canvas
39⅜ × 31⅞ inches (100 × 81 cm)
Signed lower right: *Picasso*
Signed and dated enverso: *25.3.67.II*
28031-014

PROVENANCE
Galerie Louise Leiris, Paris
Galerie Beyeler, Basel (acquired by 1981)
Private collection, Australia (acquired directly from the above in the 1980s)
Acquired by the present owner in 2008

EXHIBITED
Basel, Galerie Beyeler, *Picasso, 1881–1981. A Centennial Selection*, 1981, no. 60.
Basel, Kunstmuseum, *Pablo Picasso, Das Spätwerk*, 1981, no. 22.
Vienna, Rathaus, *Picasso in Wien*, 1981–2, no. 73.
Basel, Galerie Beyeler, *Picasso. Der Maler und seine Modelle*, 1986, no. 55.

LITERATURE
Christian Zervos, *Pablo Picasso. Oeuvres de 1965 à 1967*, Paris, 1972, vol. 25, no. 310,
    illustrated pl. 136.
The Picasso Project, *Picasso's Paintings, Watercolors, Drawings and Sculpture: The Sixties II,
    1964–1967*, San Francisco, 2002, no. 67-127, illustrated p. 306.

Le peintre belongs to a major series of paintings that Picasso executed in the late 1960s, on
the theme of the painter, which became one of the key subjects of his late *oeuvre*. The theme
of the musketeer was another major focus of his late career. By associating the persona of
the artist with that of the musketeer in *Le peintre*, Picasso reflects upon his role as an artist
and his place in the history of art. The image of the musketeer signified the golden age of
painting, revealing the influence of artists such as Rembrandt and Velazquez on Picasso's
art. Picasso had devoted a significant portion of his time and passion throughout the 1960s
to the analysis and reinterpretation of the Old Masters, during which he reaffirmed his
connection with some of the greatest painters in the history of art.

   As Marie-Laure Bernadac has observed: "If woman was depicted in all her aspects in
Picasso's art, man always appeared in disguise or in a specific role, the painter at work or
the musketeer. In 1966, a new and final character emerged in Picasso's iconography and
dominated his last period to the point of becoming its emblem. This was the Golden Age
gentleman, a half-Spanish, half-Dutch musketeer dressed in richly adorned clothing
complete with ruffs, a cape, boots, and a big plumed hat. . . . All of these musketeers are men
in disguise, romantic gentlemen, virile and arrogant soldiers, vainglorious and ridiculous
despite their haughtiness. Dressed, armed, and helmeted, this man is always seen in action;
sometimes the musketeer even takes up a brush and becomes the painter," (Brigitte Léal,
Christine Piot and Marie-Laure Bernadac, *The Ultimate Picasso*, New York, 2000, p. 455).

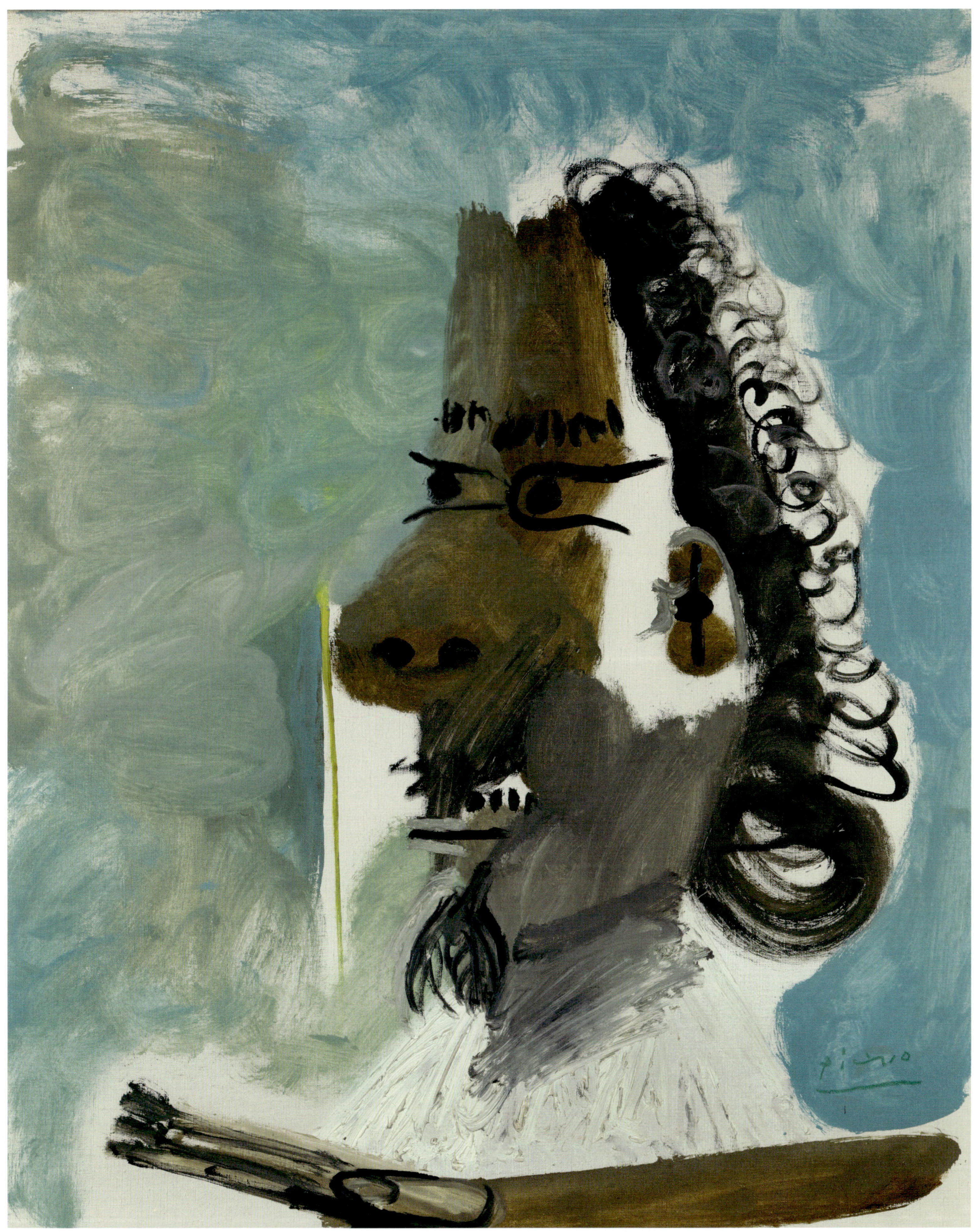

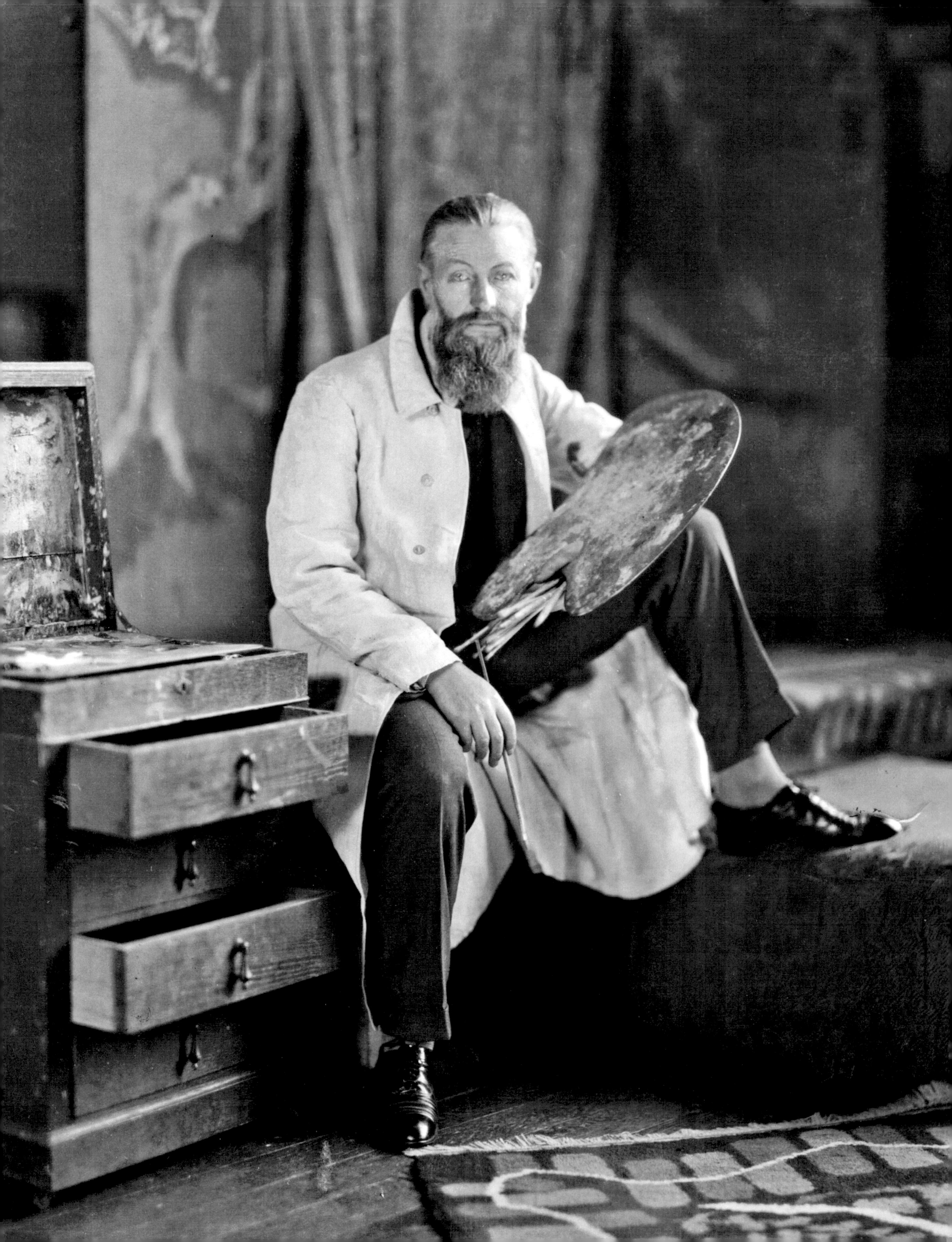

KEES VAN DONGEN (Dutch, 1877–1968)

Kees van Dongen (1877–1968) was born in Rotterdam, where he developed an early reputation for his lively drawings of the local red light district. Moving to Paris in 1899, he rapidly became associated with the circle of rebellious avant-garde artists who became known as the Fauves (or "Wild Beasts") when they exhibited together at the Salon d'Automne of 1905. In the following year he moved into the famous studio complex known as the Bateau Lavoir, where he became friends with Picasso and Picasso's then companion, Fernande Olivier. The elegant full-length portrait exhibited here, *La Parisienne de Montmartre*, belongs to this period of his activity. The townscape showing the Place Vendôme, in the heart of fashionable Paris, is, judging from the skirt-length of the figure in the foreground and the presence of early automobiles, just a little later.

Van Dongen was perhaps the first painter from the Fauve group to achieve a really solid material success. He did so through his skill as a portrait painter, and especially as a painter of fashionable women. As he rather cynically remarked, "The essential thing is to elongate the women and especially to make them slim. After that it just remains to enlarge their jewels. They are ravished." He continued to mine this particular tract of subject matter until the end of his career. One of his later works is a likeness of Brigitte Bardot, wearing an abbreviated black dress.

Because of his association with the inter-war world of high fashion, van Dongen's reputation suffered in the immediately post-war years. Recently, however, there has been a huge revival of interest in his work, culminating in an exhibition covering the earlier period of his activity that was shown at the Museum Boymans van Beuningen in Rotterdam in 2010, then again, in somewhat enlarged form, at the Musée d'Art Moderne in Paris earlier this year. Jackie Wulschlager, reviewing the Paris version of the show for the *Financial Times*, spoke of van Dongen's "obsession with women, both adored and savaged on canvas," and compared his art to that of his Dutch compatriot Willem de Kooning. Other commentators compared him to Andy Warhol, another "society painter" who managed to retain his avant-garde credentials. Because of his painterly bravura, van Dongen is once more very much in favor with collectors. His reputation now fully matches the popularity he achieved in his lifetime, when he was at the height of his fame in the 1920s.

Kees van Dongen
with his palette

KEES ᴠᴀɴ DONGEN

La Parisienne de Montmartre
Painted circa 1910
Oil on panel
29⅞ × 24¼ inches (76 × 62 cm)
Signed center right: *van Dongen*
28031-006

PROVENANCE
Charles-Auguste Marande, Le Havre
Dr. A. Roudinesco, Paris
Galleries Maurice Sternberg, Chicago
Jack Josey, Houston
Stephen Saft, Trumbull, Connecticut
Acquired by the present owner in 1990

EXHIBITED
Paris, Galerie Charpentier, *Van Dongen, oeuvres de 1890 à 1948*, 1949, March 1949, no. 25
    (as dating from 1900).
Paris, Musée National d'Art Moderne, *De Corot à nos jours au Musée du Havre*, December
    1953–January 1954, no. 93, p.21.
Paris, Galerie Charpentier, *Les Fauves*, 1962, no. 127.
Geneva, Musée Rath et Cabinet des Estampes, *Art de XXe siècle: Collections genévoises*
    June–September 1973, no.3.
Monaco, Nouveau Musée National de Monaco, *Kees van Dongen*, June 25–September 7,
    2008, no. 150, illustrated in color, p. 214; Montreal, The Montreal Museum of Fine
    Arts, January 22–April 19, 2009.

LITERATURE
Louis Chaumeil, *Van Dongen, L'homme et l'artiste—La vie et l'oeuvre*, Geneva, 1967, no. 69,
    illustrated pl. 69.

This work will be included in the forthcoming catalogue raisonné being prepared by Jacques
Chalom de Cordes under the sponsorship of the Wildenstein Institute (Ref.:99.11.2.6954.686).

Van Dongen could not resist the charms of the beautiful Pairsienne, depicting many versions of
this flamboyant character type in some of his most successful Fauvist paintings. *La Parisienne
de Montmartre* dates from the end of the artist's involvement with that avant-garde movement.
    The first owner of this picture was Charles-Auguste Marande (1858–1936), whose generous
bequest to the Malraux Museum in France accounts for a large part of their collection of
20th century art. Known to frequent the galleries of Kahnweiler, Bernheim-Jeune and Druet,
Marande built up an impressive holding of Fauvist paintings, including those of Marquet,
Camoin and van Dongen.

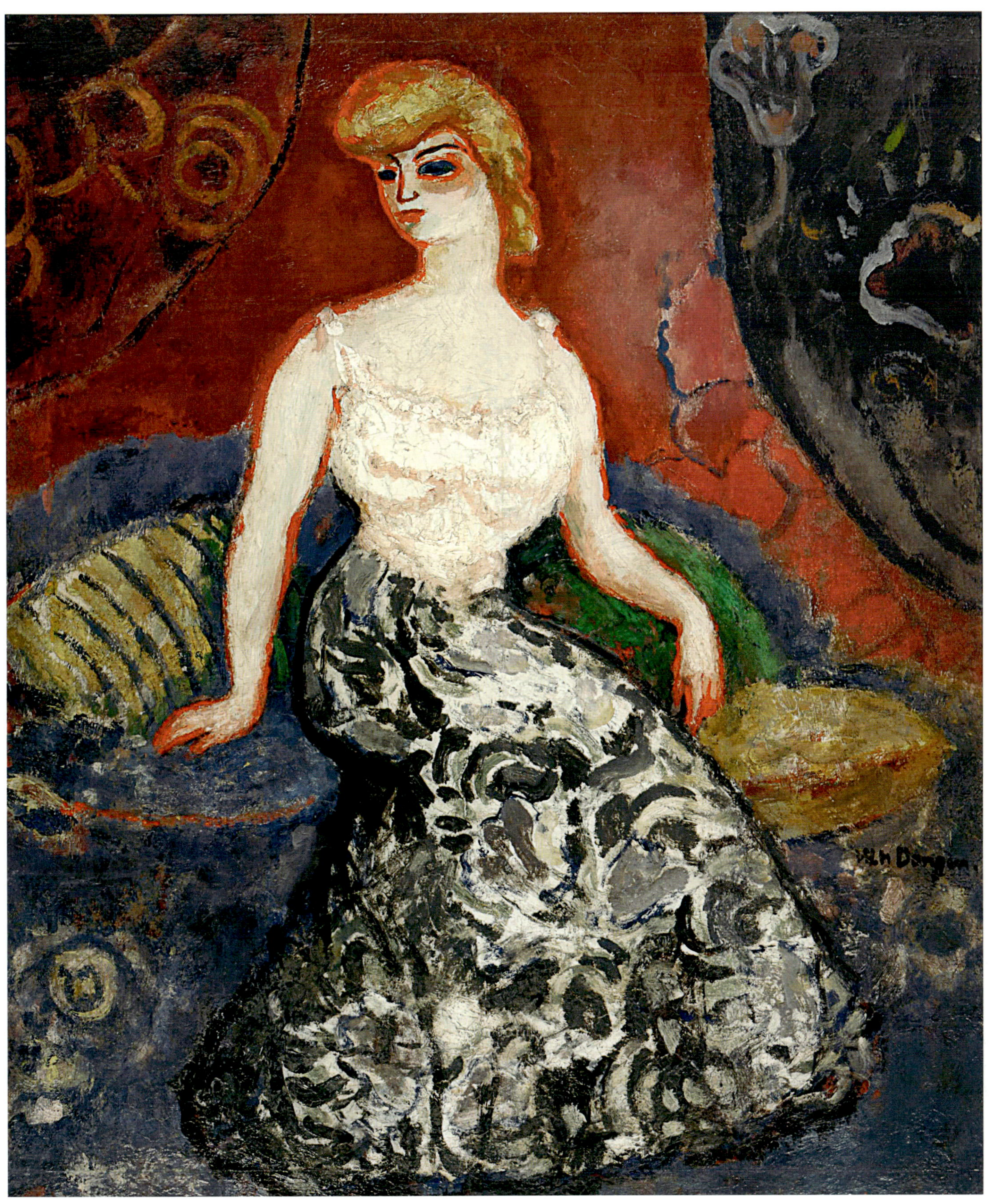

La place Vendôme
Oil on canvas
21 × 25⅝ inches (53 × 65 cm)
Signed lower right: *van Dongen*
28031-007

PROVENANCE
Galerie Maurice Chalom (acquired from the artist circa 1952)
Mr. and Mrs. Francis F. Rosenbaum, New York (acquired from the above in 1958)
Acquired by the present owner in 2004

EXHIBITED
Paris, Galerie Charpentier, 1942, no. 91 (dated 1926 and with incorrect dimensions).
Paris, Galerie Charpentier, 1949, no. 82 (dated 1913 and with incorrect dimensions).
Rotterdam, Museum Boymans Rotterdam, *Tentoonstelling, Kees van Dongen, werken
    van 1894–1949*, 1949, no. 52 (dated 1913 and with incorrect dimensions).
Paris, Musée National d'Art Moderne; Rotterdam, Boymans Van Beuningen, *Van Dongen*,
    1967–68, no. 107, illustrated.

This work will be included in the forthcoming catalogue raisonné being prepared
by Jacques Chalom de Cordes under the sponsorship of the Wildenstein Institute
(Ref.:04.03.12.9157.1875).

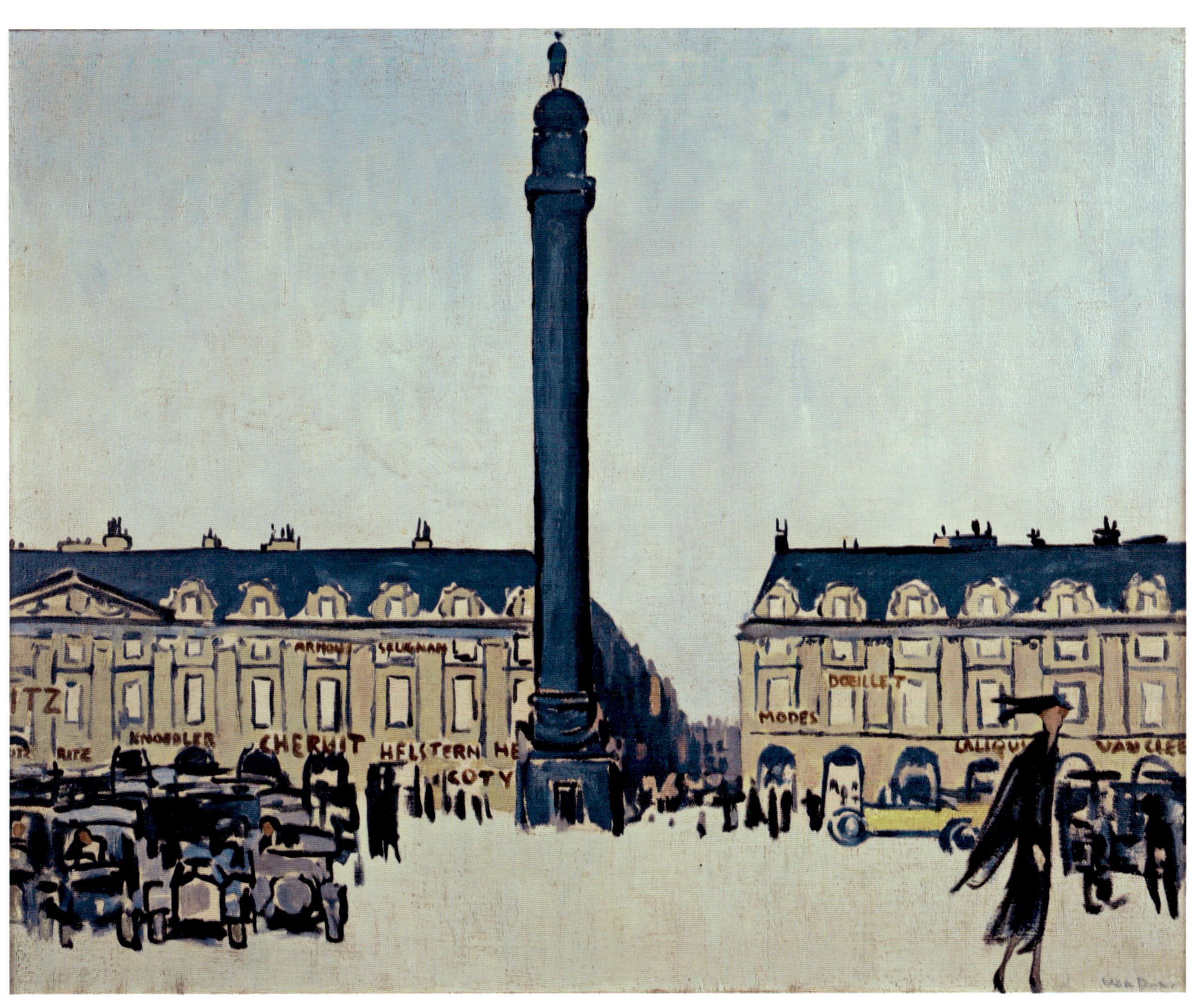

RITZ
ARNOUT SALIGNAM
KNOEDLER CHERUIT HELSTERN HE
RITZ COTY
MODES DŒILLET
LALIQUE VAN CLEE